100% Financial Literacy Success

100% Financial LITERACY SUCCESS

Gwenn Wilson

WADSWORTH
CENGAGE Learning

Australia • Brazil • Japan • Korea • Mexico • Singapore • Spain • United Kingdom • United States

100% Financial Literacy Success
Gwenn Wilson

Publisher: Lyn Uhl

Director of Developmental Studies: Annie Todd

Executive Editor: Shani Fisher

Assistant Editor: Joanna Hassel

Media Editor: Amy Gibbons

Brand Manager: Linda Yip

Content Project Manager: Cathy Brooks

Art Director: Pam Galbreath

Manufacturing Planner: Sandee Milewski

Rights Acquisition Specialist: Shalice Shah-Caldwell

Production Service and Compositor: Integra Software Services

Text Designer: Suzanne Nelson, e7 design

Cover Designer: Suzanne Nelson, e7 design

Cover Image: left, Marie C. Fields/Shutterstock.com; right, © RubberBall/Alamy

For product information and technology assistance, contact us at
Cengage Learning Customer & Sales Support, 1-800-354-9706

For permission to use material from this text or product,
submit all requests online at **www.cengage.com/permissions.**
Further permissions questions can be emailed to
permissionrequest@cengage.com.

Library of Congress Control Number: 2012943850

ISBN-13: 978-1-4354-6221-2
ISBN-10: 1-4354-6221-1

Wadsworth
20 Channel Center Street
Boston, MA 02210
USA

Cengage Learning is a leading provider of customized learning solutions with office locations around the globe, including Singapore, the United Kingdom, Australia, Mexico, Brazil and Japan. Locate your local office at **international.cengage.com/region**

Cengage Learning products are represented in Canada by Nelson Education, Ltd.

For your course and learning solutions, visit
www.cengage.com

Purchase any of our products at your local college store
or at our preferred online store **www.cengagebrain.com**

Instructors: Please visit **login.cengage.com** and log in to access instructor-specific resources.

Printed in the United States of America
1 2 3 4 5 6 7 16 15 14 13 12

Brief Table of Contents

Table of Contents

3 **PERSONAL CREDIT CARDS: GOOD OR BAD?** **57**

About the Author

GWENN WILSON, MA

Gwenn Wilson is a senior instructional designer with over 20 years of experience in Instructional Systems Design (ISD). In addition to developing academic programs and courses, Ms. Wilson has authored, edited, and reviewed textbooks and ancillary materials on a wide variety of topics. As an outside consultant, Ms. Wilson has provided training and instruction for many Fortune 500 companies in areas such as sales training, leadership training, call center training, and technical training.

Preface

HOW WILL THIS BOOK HELP ME?

Your enrollment in college says that you have made a decision to grow and develop as a person and professional. Your college experience and your future professional activities will require you to manage your personal finances in carrying out your responsibilities and achieving your professional goals. *100% Financial Literacy Success* will provide you with tools to accomplish your objectives.

100% Financial Literacy Success introduces skills that are fundamental to becoming a financially literate student and professional, which, in turn, will contribute to your academic and career success. The book focuses on the following topics: *Introduction to Financial Literacy; Learning How to Budget, Save Your Money, and Insure What You Have; Personal Credit Cards: Good or Bad?; Personal Banking; and Financial Aid Know-How;* concluding with *Understanding Taxes.* Use the following summaries of these sections to get an overview of the book and to determine how each topic supports you in the development of financial literacy skills.

▶ **INTRODUCTION TO FINANCIAL LITERACY:** It is an unfortunate fact that the number-one reason students drop out of college is because of finances. Understanding what it means to be financially literate, not just during your college career, but at any age, is the cornerstone of personal and professional success. To fully achieve financial literacy, you will also want to identify your personal values and responsibilities and your needs versus wants because this understanding helps drive your financial decisions.

▶ **LEARNING HOW TO BUDGET, SAVE YOUR MONEY, AND INSURE WHAT YOU HAVE:** While it may sound straightforward and necessary, learning how to effectively create, adhere to, and adjust a personal budget is the first step to achieving financial literacy. In concert with this critical piece is gaining an understanding of how to save money and how that impacts your budgeting process. Additional information about the types of insurance you should carry will help you protect what you have worked to attain.

▶ **PERSONAL CREDIT CARDS: GOOD OR BAD?:** Getting a credit card (or cards) can be relatively easy today. The hard part of owning one is learning to be responsible and frugal in its use. While there are many advantages to owning a credit card, such as establishing a good credit rating, real and potentially long-lasting consequences can result from mismanaging this personal financial tool.

▶ **PERSONAL BANKING:** Understanding personal banking can help you achieve your financial goals. This includes which type of bank and banking services best fit your needs. Learn what choices you have so that you can make informed decisions when it comes to your money.

▶ **FINANCIAL AID KNOW-HOW:** The overarching purpose of financial aid is to help you in your quest to pursue your academic and professional careers. But how do you navigate the myriad of choices when it comes to choosing the financial aid option(s) that work best for you? A discussion of the financial alternatives that may be available to you sheds light on this process. Guidance on how to complete the Free Application for Federal Student Aid (FAFSA) and other financial forms is also included.

Student loans are just one type of financial aid, but within this one category there are many different choices at the federal, state, and private level. A thorough dialogue on student loans will help guide you into good decision making when it comes to securing one or more loans in your lifetime.

▶ **UNDERSTANDING TAXES:** Personal taxes represent another financial maze that is often difficult to understand and that can carry significant penalties if not properly handled. A fundamental knowledge of your obligations and responsibilities in this arena will help to ensure that you don't get caught in the "tax trap."

HOW TO USE THIS BOOK

100% Financial Literacy Success is designed to actively involve you in developing financial literacy skills. The book includes the following features that will guide you through the material and provide opportunities for you to practice what you've learned.

▶ **LEARNING OBJECTIVES:** Learning Objectives, like those provided on course syllabi, are provided to outline what you should be learning from the chapter and guide you to the main concepts of the chapter. Use the objectives to identify important points and to understand what you are supposed to learn, to measure what you have mastered, and to identify what you still need to work on. You are encouraged to expand your knowledge beyond the learning objectives according to your goals and interests.

▶ **CASE IN POINT:** At the beginning of each chapter, a case study demonstrates the application of chapter concepts to the real world. Use the questions following each case study to stimulate your critical thinking and analytical skills. Discuss the questions with classmates. You are encouraged to think of your own application of ideas and to raise additional questions.

▶ **CRITICAL THINKING QUESTIONS:** The Critical Thinking Questions challenge you to examine ideas and thoughtfully apply concepts presented in the book. These questions encourage the development of thinking skills that are crucial for efficient performance in school and in the workplace.

▶ *SUCCESS STEPS:* Scattered throughout the book are Success Steps that offer a pathway to achieve various goals. They essentially summarize the detailed processes that are discussed fully in the body of the book. To achieve a specific financial literacy goal, use the *Table of Contents* to locate the information quickly.

▶ **APPLY IT!:** At the end of each chapter are activities that will help you apply the concepts discussed in practical situations. Your instructor may assign these activities as part of the course requirements. Or, if they are not formally assigned, you will want to complete them for your own development:

- *Individual Activities* are directed at your personal development.

- *Group Activities* typically include projects that are completed more successfully from several perspectives or broader research. As the title suggests, a team effort will contribute to the success of these learning projects. You may find it helpful to combine individual and group activities. Some individual activities can be adapted to group activities and vice versa. Use the activities as guides and modify them in ways that best support your learning.

- *Internet Activities* are intended to help you develop online skills. For example, you may be asked to research a topic using online resources.

ANCILLARY MATERIALS

The **Student Companion Site** includes practice quizzes, flash cards, exercises, a glossary of terms, and additional resources to help students be successful in their course. Students can access this free Web site at www.cengagebrain.com.

The **Instructor's Companion Site** includes an Instructor's Manual, PowerPoint Slides, Sample Syllabi, and a Test Bank. Access the Instructor Companion Site by logging into your account at http://login.cengage.com. A **WebTutor Toolbox** is also available for use with WebCT or Blackboard.

College Success Factors Index (CSFI) 2.0 is an online survey that students complete to assess their patterns and behavior in 10 factors that are specific to succeeding in the classroom/campus: Responsibility/Control, Competition, Task Planning, Expectations, Wellness, Time Management, College Involvement, Family Involvement, Precision, and Persistence. The CSFI is a perfect assessment tool for tracking your students' success in the course. For more information about this resource, visit www.cengage.com/success/csfi2.

The **College Success Planner** is an annual planner available as a package item with this textbook. This 18-month planner assists students in making the best use of their time both on and off campus.

An additional service available with this textbook is support from **TeamUP Faculty Program Consultants.** For more than a decade, our consultants have helped faculty reach and engage first-year students by offering peer-to-peer consulting on curriculum and assessment, faculty training, and workshops. Consultants are available to help you establish or improve our student success program and provide training on the implementation of our textbooks and technology. To connect with your TeamUP Faculty Program Consultant, call 1-800-528-8323 or visit www.cengage.com/teamup.

For more in-depth information on any of these items, talk with your sales rep, or visit www.cengagebrain.com.

ACKNOWLEDGMENTS

The author would like to extend a special acknowledgment to the following instructors for their reviews that helped mold the ideas for the first edition of this book:

Paula Walker, Heritage College and Heritage Institute
Scott Allen, IADT-Seattle
Patricia Hollander, ASA
Tony Aponte, IADT
Eleanor Sweetwood, IADT Seattle

100% Financial Literacy Success

Andresr/Shutterstock.com

CHAPTER OUTLINE

Financial Literacy Defined

The Importance of Financial Literacy at Any Age

Personal Values and Personal Responsibilities

The Seven Levels of Maslow's Hierarchy of Needs

Getting Started on Your Financial Journey and How Technology Can Help

1 Introduction to Financial Literacy

THE BIG PICTURE

This chapter lays the foundation for understanding the many aspects of financial literacy. It also provides a context for applying the information presented in subsequent chapters.

LEARNING OBJECTIVES

By the end of this chapter, you will achieve the following objectives:

▶ Define *financial literacy*.

▶ Explain the importance of being financially literate at any age.

▶ Distinguish between personal values and personal responsibilities.

▶ Identify the seven levels of Maslow's Hierarchy of Needs.

▶ Explain how technology aids in achieving financial literacy.

1

CHAPTER 1 CASE IN POINT

Lauren Bishop is an incoming freshman at a college one state away from where she grew up. This is her first time away from home without the daily guidance of her parents.

While still in high school, Lauren worked part-time at a local gourmet shop assisting customers and stocking merchandise. Although her earnings were relatively small, Lauren's parents insisted that she open a checking account at the local bank so that she could learn "the ropes" of managing her money and how to use a debit card. While she is at school, Lauren's parents are going to use that checking account to give Lauren a monthly budgeted amount to fund items that are not paid for by other means.

During freshman orientation on campus, Lauren noticed a hub of activity at the student union where vendors were peddling a variety of services, among them several credit card companies offering such incentives as a free T-shirt, a Frisbee, or 10 percent off their first purchase, simply by filling out a credit card application. Enticed by that 10-percent discount and the notion of being an "adult" with a "real" credit card, Lauren filled out the application and waited for her card to arrive in the mail.

When the credit card arrived in her dorm mailbox a short time later, she immediately went to the local mall to purchase a sweater like the ones so many young women on campus were wearing that fall. She figured that she could pay her credit card bill from her checking account when the statement arrived 30 days later and not tell her parents about it.

Unfortunately for Lauren, when the card statement arrived, she did not have enough money in her checking account to cover the cost of the sweater. In addition, the credit card company had tacked on a twenty-five-dollar annual fee that Lauren had not anticipated. Lauren decided that the best thing to do would be to pay the minimum amount required that month while hoping she would have sufficient funds next month to bring the balance to zero.

Imagine yourself to be in Lauren's position. Thoughtfully and honestly answer the following questions:

▶ How dependent are you on others for your financial well-being?

▶ How well do you think you manage your personal finances?

continued

> Do you take full responsibility for your financial situation?
> How do you decide if a purchase is something you need or want?
> How do you rate yourself when it comes to understanding the use of credit cards?
> From whom do you seek financial advice?

FINANCIAL LITERACY DEFINED

In these tough and uncertain economic times, many Americans find themselves struggling to make ends meet, often living paycheck to paycheck. The average citizen confronts mounting debt, is unclear about how to make important financial decisions, and will experience a later and less secure retirement. Financial problems such as these can lead to health issues, emotional stress, and decreased productivity (Shorb, n.d.). While this current phenomenon has many causes, a major contributing factor is that many Americans are *financially illiterate*.

Financial illiteracy in this country is not unique to one gender, socioeconomic group, age, or race. It impacts Americans in a variety of ways, all of them negatively. Consider the following:

> **LACK OF SAVINGS AND DEBT.** A failure to save, or save sufficiently, can affect one's financial circumstances. Using credit, and thus carrying debt, to "fix" financial problems leads to even greater financial consequences.

> **BANKRUPTCY AND FORECLOSURE.** Financial illiteracy has led many Americans down the unfortunate path of severe financial problems, including bankruptcy and foreclosure.

> **INCREASE IN EXPENSES.** A lack of financial literacy causes people to make misinformed choices that can cost large amounts of money in terms of interest payments over time.

moshimochi/Shutterstock.com

Learning the ropes of financial literacy now will bode well for you the rest of your life.

▶ **WORKPLACE ISSUES.** Financial stress at home can find its way into the workplace, thus impacting productivity and creating increased emotional stress.

▶ **HEALTH AND RELATIONSHIPS.** Money issues can creep into other aspects of our lives, often negatively, potentially affecting one's health, employment, and relationships (Shorb, n.d.).

WHAT IS FINANCIAL LITERACY?

So, then, what can we do as Americans to remove ourselves from the path of the oncoming train that is financial illiteracy? The answer, of course, is to become financially literate. But what does that term mean, and how does one go about becoming financially literate?

In the *2008 Annual Report to the President* as authored by the President's Advisory Council on Financial Literacy, the Council defines **financial literacy** as "the ability to use knowledge and skills to manage financial resources effectively for a lifetime of financial well-being." Further, the Council defines **financial education** as "the process by which people improve their understanding of financial products, services, and concepts, so they are empowered to make informed choices, avoid pitfalls, know where to go for help and take other actions to improve their present and long-term financial well-being" (Department of the Treasury, 2008).

As a college student, you are a possible candidate for accumulating debt through the use of student loans, credit cards, and making financial missteps that can cause you real financial harm, now and well into your adult life. As you transition from college into the workplace, you will be exposed to numerous choices of financial services and products, more so than you are now, and mistakes at this level can have significant ramifications, including job loss, a poor credit rating, bankruptcy, and even homelessness.

If you haven't started already, *now* is the time to begin your financial education so that you can achieve financial literacy that will serve you at present and well into your future.

THE IMPORTANCE OF FINANCIAL LITERACY AT ANY AGE

As you embark on your journey to financial literacy, it's important to establish a baseline of what you know you know, what you think you know, what you think you might not know, and what you know you don't know about personal finances and money management. In this way, you can target the areas in which you need to shore up your financial education.

Let's begin with a simple "Financial Aptitude Test," as provided by the Federal Deposit Insurance Corporation (FDIC) that will help you to gauge your financial education.

1. It's always smart to send in the minimum payment due on a credit card bill each month and stretch out the card payments as long as possible instead of paying the bill in full. *True or False?*

2. Your credit record (your history of paying debts and other bills) can be a factor when you apply for a loan or a credit card but cannot affect noncredit decisions such as applications for insurance or an apartment. *True or False?*

3. While one or two late payments on bills may not damage your credit record, making a habit of it will count against you. *True or False?*

4. There's no harm in having many different credit cards, especially when the card companies offer free T-shirts and other special giveaways as incentives. The number of cards you carry won't affect your ability to get a loan; what matters is that you use the cards responsibly. *True or False?*

5. A debit card may be a good alternative to a credit card for a young person because the money to pay for purchases is automatically deducted from a bank account, thus avoiding interest charges or debt problems. *True or False?*

6. It makes no sense for young adults to put money aside for their retirement many years away. People in their 20s should focus entirely on meeting monthly expenses and

saving for short-term goals (such as buying a home or starting a business) and not start saving for retirement until their 40s at the earliest. *True or False?*

7. If you receive an e-mail from a company you've done business with asking you to update your records by reentering your Social Security number or bank account numbers, it's safe to provide this information as long as the e-mail explains the reason for the request and shows the company's official logo. *True or False?*

8. The best way to avoid a "bounced" check—that is, a check that gets rejected by your financial institution because you've overdrawn your account—is to keep your checkbook up to date and closely monitor your balance. Institutions do offer "overdraft-protection" services, but these programs come with their own costs. *True or False?*

9. All checking accounts are pretty much the same in terms of features, fees, interest rates, opening balance requirements, and so on. *True or False?*

10. Let's say you put money in a savings account paying the same interest rate each month, and you don't take any money out. Even though your original deposit and the interest rate remain unchanged, the amount of money you will earn in interest each month will gradually increase. *True or False?* (Federal Deposit Insurance Corporation, 2005).

Note: Answer key to Financial Aptitude Test is located on page 29.

Obviously this "test" is not all encompassing, nor was it designed to be. But it should give you an indication of topic areas where you might want to put some additional thought or do some research on your own.

Activity #1: Self-Analysis: Grading Your Financial Acumen, found at the end of this chapter, will help guide you in assessing your strengths and weaknesses when it comes to your financial education.

IT'S NOT TOO EARLY TO START SAVING

Ideally, the road to financial literacy should start at an early age and continue as a lifelong journey. Unfortunately, most of us do not start on this road until we are adults; oftentimes we do not save enough to be financially secure, let alone enjoy a comfortable retirement.

As a young college student, you should be aware that one of the first tenets of sound financial decision making is to abide by the concept of "pay yourself first." By this we mean automatically putting some money into a savings account or other investments such as a U.S. Savings Bond before you are tempted to spend it. Start small, even if it's just twenty-five or fifty dollars a month. If you have those funds automatically deducted from your paycheck and placed into savings, you won't miss them. "The important thing is to start saving as early as you can—even saving for retirement when that seems light years away—so you can benefit from the effect of compound interest," states Donna Gambrell, of the FDIC's Division of Supervision and Consumer Protection (Federal Deposit Insurance Corporation, 2005). **Compound interest** is when interest on an investment (such as money in a savings account) itself earns interest.

Another way to save money is by not falling into the trap of common mistakes that young adults tend to make with their money. Certainly everyone makes financial mistakes at one or more points in their lives, but the trick is to keep those mistakes at a minimum, and, even more important, to learn from them. This is a significant facet of your financial education and one that you are wise to learn from sooner rather than later.

The following list includes top financial mistakes that many young people make and what you can do to avoid making those mistakes from the start:

▶ **PURCHASING ITEMS YOU DON'T NEED AND PAYING EXTRA FOR THEM IN INTEREST.** Think back to the Case in Point at the beginning of this chapter. Lauren Bishop used her credit card to pay for a sweater, only to find out that she didn't have enough money in her checking account to pay off the balance. Only paying the minimum amount guarantees that Lauren will incur finance charges in the coming month (and perhaps for many months to follow). So how do you avoid Lauren's situation? Consider the following:

• Really assess if you "need" the item versus "want" the item. Try not to bow to peer pressure or to reward yourself if

1

things are going well or not so well. Impulse buying can make you feel good for the moment, but it won't make you feel so great when that credit card statement comes calling. Waiting a day or two, or even just a few hours, before you purchase (and be mindful of how quick and easy it is to shop online) may prevent you from making a costly decision that you will come to regret.

- Research major purchases and comparison shop before you buy. Doing so will not only get you the best deal for your money; it also might sway your decision against making the purchase at all.

- If you do use a credit card to pay for a major purchase, be smart about how you repay. If available, take advantage of offers of "zero-percent interest" on credit card purchases for a certain number of months. Be mindful, however, of when and how interest charges begin and what that does to your monthly payment amount. Always pay as much as you can before interest charges kick in so that you are paying interest on a lower balance than the purchase price.

▶ **GETTING TOO DEEPLY INTO DEBT.** Sure, this seems obvious. Don't spend what you don't have. That's simple, right? Unfortunately, our ability to borrow (via credit cards and other means) is all too easy these days. And borrowing helps us get what we want, when we want it. With this reality comes the fact that millions of adults of all ages find themselves struggling to pay their loans, credit cards, and other bills. Learn to be a good money manager and to recognize the warning signs of a serious debt problem. Some of these warning signs include the following:

- Borrowing money to make payments on loans you already have

- Getting payday loans. A **payday loan** (also called a **paycheck advance**) is a small, short-term loan that is intended to cover a borrower's expenses until his or her next payday.

- Deliberately paying your bills late

- Putting off doctor visits or other important life activities because you don't have enough money

▶ **TARNISHING YOUR FINANCIAL REPUTATION.** The simplest way around this is to pay your bills on time, every month. While one or two late payments on your loans or other regular financial obligations (rent, for example) will probably not hurt you in the long run, a pattern of late bill payment can adversely affect your **credit score**s and **credit report**. Here's how that can happen:

- **Credit bureau**s are companies that prepare credit reports used by lenders, employers, insurance companies, and others to assess your financial reliability, generally based on your track record of paying bills and debts. They produce credit scores that evaluate a person's credit record based on a point system. If your credit scores are low and your credit report is damaged by your inability to pay your bills on time, you will likely be charged a higher interest rate on your credit card(s) or on a loan that you really want and need. You could also be turned down for employment or renting an apartment. Even your auto insurance may be negatively impacted.

▶ **YOU OWN A FISTFUL OF CREDIT CARDS.** The general rule of thumb is that two to four credit cards are a sufficient amount for most adults. These include any cards from department stores, oil companies, and any other retailers. Why shouldn't you carry more than this suggested amount?

- Temptation, plain and simple. The more cards you have, the more tempted you may be to use them to fuel costly impulse buying.

- Each card you own, even if you don't use it, represents money that you *could* borrow up to the card's **spending limit**. For each new card you acquire, you are seen as someone who could potentially get into greater debt. And that could mean qualifying for a smaller or costlier loan.

▶ **NOT TRACKING YOUR EXPENSES.** It's easy to overspend in some areas, most likely for the things you want (not necessarily need), and to shortchange other areas, including that savings account that you were so good about opening. Devising a tracking/budget system that works for you is your best bet for setting and sticking to your financial limits.

▶ **WATCH OUT FOR THOSE FEES.** Financial institutions love to charge noncustomers anywhere from one dollar to four dollars for using their automated teller machines (ATMs). They are also quick to charge for **bounced check**s, that is, writing checks for more than you have in your account. These fees can range from 15 to 30 dollars for *each* check. You can take the following steps to mitigate these unwanted fees:

- Whenever possible, use your financial institution's ATMs (including branches) or ATMs that are a part of an ATM network to which your bank belongs.

- To avoid bounced check fees, keep your checkbook balanced and up to date, including recording all debit card transactions. This task becomes easier with the use of online and phone banking, both of which are free services. In addition, be sure to record those ATM withdrawal slips within your check register or cross-reference them online. If not closely monitored, those unrecorded $20 ATM transactions can result in your account being overdrawn (Federal Deposit Insurance Corporation, 2005).

We will discuss all of these suggestions for minimizing financial mistakes throughout the remainder of this textbook.

SEEKING FINANCIAL ADVICE

Ultimately, it is you who must take charge of your finances. But as we have already seen, successfully managing one's financial situation can be a daunting task, with many risks (and rewards, it is hoped!) associated with it. The good news is that even though you hold final responsibility for your finances, there are people, companies, and government agencies that can help you in your financial decision making, now and well into your future.

People get their money advice from myriad sources. At your age, your main source of financial advice may come from your parents. Studies corroborate that most young adults today rely on their parents as the main source of financial knowledge (Shorb, n.d.). The good news is that parents are seen as a trusted source of information. The bad news is that if parents exhibit bad financial habits, those habits most likely are passed down to the next generation.

Here are some resources you can tap into to get financial advice:

▶ **FAMILY, FRIENDS, AND COWORKERS.** The caveat here is that while you trust and admire these people, they really might not be very financially literate themselves.

▶ **YOUR FINANCIAL INSTITUTION.** Every bank and credit union has people on staff who can give you advice on the services they offer that best meet your financial needs, including the merits of online banking. They can also provide you with written materials on a variety of topics that you can use for reference. Their web sites also contain useful information.

▶ **YOUR SCHOOL.** Check with the Financial Aid office for information on student loans, grants, scholarships, loan repayment information, **exit counseling**, and other financial information. The Career Services office has both onsite and online resources available to you, including data on internships, job searches, networking, and other career counseling information. (Read more about the Financial Aid office in Chapter 5 of this textbook.)

▶ **GOVERNMENT AGENCIES.** Many federal and state government agencies are dedicated to financial information geared to consumers. Most of the information is available via agency web sites. Some of the most useful ones include the following:

• **The Federal Deposit Insurance Corporation (FDIC)** web site at www.fdic.gov/consumers. The FDIC Consumer Protection page provides a wealth of financial information to educate and protect consumers on a wide variety of topics, including banking and your money, loans and mortgages, identity theft and fraud, and updated consumer news.

• **The Financial Literacy and Education Commission** web site at www.mymoney.gov. MyMoney.gov is the U.S. government's web site dedicated to teaching all Americans the basics about financial education. The site houses important information from 20 federal agencies and bureaus designed to help consumers make smart financial choices.

• **360 Degrees of Financial Literacy** web site at www.360financialliteracy.org. Sponsored by the American Institute of Certified Public Accountants, the site is intended to help Americans understand their personal finances through every stage of life. This site has a page dedicated to college students.

- **Your state's official** web site. Most state governments offer assistance and publish useful information for its citizens, including how to start a business, labor and employment information, and tax information.

▶ **YOUR EMPLOYER.** Many employers, especially larger ones, offer investment opportunities through stock purchase plans, 401K programs, and the like. The Human Resources department generally has printed materials and might offer classes to help you make informed investment decisions.

▶ **THE MEDIA.** The Internet, newspapers and magazines, television, and radio are filled with information about financial matters. When accessing information via the Internet, bear in mind that anyone can put anything up on the World Wide Web, and not all sources are reliable or trustworthy. Generally, you can rely on the .gov and .edu web sites as being reliable and presenting relatively accurate information. The government or educational entity behind the site is usually bound by a code of ethics and is watched by many different individuals or agencies. Regardless, be sure to verify your source(s) before moving forward with any financial decisions or taking the information as truth.

▶ **EDUCATIONAL OPPORTUNITIES.** Consult your local library, schools, community college, and other educational resources for personal finance classes, seminars, and the like. Financial institutions and those in the "money business" (investment bankers, brokers, financial advisors, and so on) often sponsor discussions on different financial vehicles and investment opportunities.

▶ **FINANCIAL PLANNER.** A **financial planner** is an investment professional who helps individuals set and achieve their long-term financial goals. The role of a financial planner is to find ways to increase the client's net worth and help the client accomplish all of their financial objectives. As a college student, you might not need this level of financial advice, but you might want to seek the advice of such a person as you enter the

1

workforce, purchase a home, start a family, and so on. Note that using a financial planner costs money.

success steps for seeking financial advice

- Enlist the help of family, friends, and coworkers.
- Speak to staff members at your financial institution.
- Tap into resources at your school.
- Check the web sites of federal and state government agencies that provide financial guidance.
- Consult with your employer on retirement and investment opportunities.
- Use different media outlets to conduct research on financial issues.
- Take advantage of any financial educational opportunities in your area.
- Seek out the counsel of a financial planner.

PERSONAL VALUES AND PERSONAL RESPONSIBILITIES

Thinking about and discovering what you want out of life gives you guidance for what to do to lead a satisfying life. Understanding yourself enables you to make key life decisions. One of the significant steps in this process is to identify your personal values.

Personal values are the principles, standards, or qualities individuals consider worthwhile or desirable. Values provide a basis for decisions about how to live and serve as guides we can use to direct our actions. For something to be of value, it must be prized, publically affirmed, chosen from alternatives, and acted on repeatedly and consistently. Values are not right or wrong or true or false; they are personal preferences.

People may place value on family, friends, helping others, religious commitment, honesty, pleasure, good health, material possessions,

1

The financial road you choose to travel says much about your understanding of financial literacy.

financial security, and a satisfying career. Examples of conflicting values are family versus satisfying career, religious beliefs versus pleasure, and material possessions versus financial security (Garman and Forgue, 2010). If you are unsure of, or lose sight of your values, you fall into the trap of making choices out of impulse or instant gratification rather than on sound reasoning and responsible decision making (Hereford, n.d.).

Closely aligned with personal values is the concept of responsibility and personal responsibility. "Responsibility means being accountable for what we think, say, and do. **Personal responsibility** involves working on our own character and skill development rather than blaming others for situations and circumstances. It means choosing to design a life that honors our values and purpose," states professional life success coach Steve Brunkhorst. Accepting personal responsibility is what moves you from childhood into adulthood. It is part of the maturation process that you are undergoing at this stage of your life. Personal responsibility does not stand alone, however. It influences your successes, achievements, motivation, happiness, and self-actualization. By accepting that you are wholly responsible for yourself and that no one—neither your parents, your teachers, nor your friends—is coming to your rescue, signals that you have become an adult (Tracy, n.d.).

RESPONSIBILITIES VERSUS EXCUSES

On the other end of the spectrum are excuses, the polar opposite of personal responsibility. Excuses allow you to blame others for what's happening in your life. They rob you of your ability to achieve your goals, and they steal your self-esteem and quality of life (Bowman, n.d.).

Excuses are also habit forming. If you get into the habit of making excuses, you have also fallen into the trap of avoiding responsibility at the same time. It's easy to set a goal or objective for yourself and even easier to create an excuse as a "just-in-case" fallback in the event that it is too hard for you to accomplish that goal (Tracy, n.d.).

PERSONAL VALUES VERSUS FINANCIAL GOALS

So far in this book, we have seen several examples of how people tend to be financially illiterate, and we've identified many common financial mistakes that young adults make. One of the most important steps you can take as you journey down the road to financial literacy is to understand the relationship between your personal values and your financial goals.

As we have seen, values provide a basis for decisions about how to live and serve as guides we can use to direct our actions. **Goals** are the vehicle for putting those actions into motion.

Successful financial planning evolves from your financial goals. **Financial goals** are the specific short-, medium-, and long-term objectives that you want to attain through financial planning and management efforts. Financial goals should be consistent with your personal values (Garman and Forgue, 2010). As a young adult, you may define short-, medium-, and long-term goals in these time frames:

▶ **SHORT-TERM.** Goals that can be accomplished in three months or fewer. As an example of this, you might want to save $100 to buy an e-reader in three months.

▶ **MEDIUM-TERM.** Goals that will take between three months and one year to achieve. For example, you might like to save for six months to take a trip with friends next summer.

▶ **LONG-TERM.** Goals that take more than one year to accomplish. One of your long-term goals following graduation could be to pay off your student loans early by paying an extra $150 per month (CashCourse, 2011[b]).

1

Setting goals helps you visualize the gap between your current financial status and where you want to be in the future. Examples of financial goals include the following:

▶ Finish a college education.

▶ Pay off education loans.

▶ Take a vacation.

▶ Own a home.

▶ Meet financial emergencies.

▶ Accumulate funds to send children through college.

▶ Be financially independent at retirement.

None of these goals, however, is specific enough to guide financial behavior. Specific goals should be measurable, attainable, realistic, and time-bound (Garman and Forgue, 2010).

Consider the following acronym when goal setting. Turn your goals into SMART goals. SMART goals are Specific, Measurable, Attainable, Realistic, and Time-bound. This provides you with a plan that has a sequence of achievable small steps that will lead to you reaching your goals, financial or otherwise.

Let's say one of your medium-term goals is to go with your friends to Colorado next July for a week. Make this a SMART goal by doing the following:

▶ **SPECIFIC:** A specific goal is, "I want to spend a week next summer in Colorado with three friends." A vague goal, for comparison, is more like stating, "I want to do something fun next summer."

▶ **MEASURABLE:** You need $500 for your share of gas money for the drive to Colorado and back, your share of the split hotel room cost, and food for the week. This is more concrete than "I will need money for the trip."

▶ **ATTAINABLE:** It's February, so you have about five months to save for your trip in July, and you'll save the money from your campus bookstore job. You need to save $100 per month, or $25 per week, to go on the trip. You are more apt to see results with this goal than if you say, "I'll save any money that's left over at the end of the month."

▶ **REALISTIC:** You and your friends will drive the 1000 miles in 15 hours, splitting driving time among the four of you. A vague goal is more like saying, "We'll make the trip in a day."

▶ **TIME-BOUND:** You'll have 75 percent of the money saved by May. A vague goal would be to say, "I'll have the money by mid-Spring" (CashCourse, 2011[a]).

Setting your own financial goals is not rocket science, but it is on the critical path to achieving financial literacy. Take the time now to write down your goals, revisit them often, accomplish them, and then create new goals to help ensure your financial well-being now and well into the later stages of your life.

THE SEVEN LEVELS OF MASLOW'S HIERARCHY OF NEEDS

Abraham Maslow was a psychologist who in the 1940s introduced the concept of a "hierarchy of needs" as an explanation of a person's growth and development as that person works to achieve their full potential. Usually presented as a pyramid (see Figure 1-1), the hierarchy suggests that people are motivated to fulfill the most basic of needs first before moving on to other needs (Cherry, n.d.).

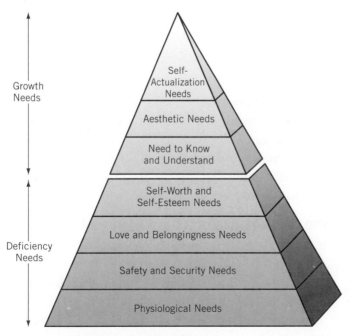

Figure 1-1   Maslow's Hierarchy of Needs.

Source: Text Material adapted from D. Martin and K. Joomis, *Building Teachers: A Constructivist Approach to Introducing Education,* (Belmont, CA: Wadsworth, 2007), pp. 72-75

TYPES OF NEEDS

As you can see, the lowest levels of the pyramid comprise a person's most basic needs, while the top of the pyramid denotes more complex needs. Maslow believed that a person's needs are similar to instincts and that they play a significant role in motivating human behavior (Cherry, n.d.). The lowest four needs—physiological, safety and security, love and belongingness, and self-worth and self-esteem—are considered deficiency needs (also known as D-needs), essential for a person's well-being. These needs must be satisfied before the person is motivated to seek experiences that pertain to the upper levels (Martin and Joomis, 2007).

The top three layers of the pyramid—the need to know and understand, aesthetic needs, and the need for self-actualization—are considered growth needs (sometimes referred to as being needs or B-needs). Growth needs can never be satisfied completely. Contrary to the deficiency needs, for which motivation diminishes when a need is satisfied, as growth needs are met, people's motivation to meet additional growth needs increases. The more these needs are satisfied, the more people want to pursue them. For example, the more one comes to understand, the more one's motivation to learn more increases (Martin and Joomis, 2007). Detailed information on each of the seven levels follows:

▶ **PHYSIOLOGICAL NEEDS.** Maslow suggested that the first and most basic need people have is the need for survival: their physiological requirements for food, water, and shelter. People must have food to eat, water to drink, and a place to call home before they can think about anything else. If any of these physiological necessities is missing, people are motivated above all else to meet that missing need.

▶ **SAFETY AND SECURITY NEEDS.** After their physiological needs have been satisfied, people can work to meet their needs for safety and security. (But the physiological needs must be met first.) Safety is the feeling people get when they know no harm will befall them physically, mentally, or emotionally; security is the feeling people get when their fears and anxieties are low.

▶ **LOVE AND BELONGINGNESS NEEDS.** After the physiological needs and the needs for survival and for safety and security have been met, an individual can be motivated to meet the needs represented at higher levels of the pyramid. The third level of the pyramid represents needs associated with love and belonging. These needs are met through satisfactory relationships—relationships with family members, friends, peers, classmates, teachers, and other people with whom individuals interact. Satisfactory relationships imply acceptance by others. Having satisfied their physiological and security needs, people can venture out and seek relationships from which their need for love and belonging can be met.

▶ **SELF-WORTH AND SELF-ESTEEM NEEDS.** Once individuals have satisfactorily met their need for love and belonging, they can begin to develop positive feelings of self-worth and self-esteem and act to foster pride in their work and in themselves as people. Before they can work toward self-esteem, however, they must feel safe, secure, and part of a group such as a class in school.

▶ **NEED TO KNOW AND UNDERSTAND.** The fifth level of Maslow's pyramid represents an individual's need to know and understand. According to Maslow's hierarchy, this motivation cannot occur until the deficiency needs have been met to the individual's satisfaction.

▶ **AESTHETIC NEEDS. Aesthetics** refers to the quality of being creatively, beautifully, or artistically pleasing; aesthetic needs are the needs to express oneself in pleasing ways. People are motivated to meet this need only after the previous five needs have been met.

▶ **NEED FOR SELF-ACTUALIZATION.** At the top of the pyramid is the need for **self-actualization**, which is a person's desire to become everything he or she is capable of becoming—to realize and use his or her full potential, capacities, and talents. This need can be addressed only when the previous six have been satisfied. It is rarely met completely; Maslow (1968) estimated that fewer than 1 percent of adults achieve total self-actualization (Martin and Joomis, 2007).

1

DISTINGUISHING BETWEEN NEEDS AND WANTS

One of the hardest things we learn as we grow up is how to understand the difference between a "need" and a "want." A **need** is something that is a necessity in life, such as food, water, and shelter. A **want** is something that is not a necessity but is desired to increase the quality of life. As you move into adulthood, it's very important that you have a clear understanding of these two terms and how they directly impact your financial well-being.

To look at it another way, a need is a "have to have" and a want is a "nice to have." So, for example, you may need a new pair of sneakers, but wanting the athlete-endorsed pair at three times the cost of a regular pair can get you into financial trouble, especially if it is at the expense of some of your identified needs. That's where so many young adults get into debt. The *want factor* overrides the *need factor*, and so out comes the credit card, or the failure to pay established bills, or dipping into savings (if there *are* savings), all of which are used to fulfill a want, not a need.

As Maslow's hierarchy of needs points out, motivation in life is key. When the first four levels of the pyramid, the deficiency needs, are met, motivation diminishes. You have food and shelter, you are safe and secure, you are loved and feel a part of a larger circle, and you have a measure of self-worth and self-esteem. It's all good, as they say. It's the status quo.

As a young person embarking on your adult life, now is the time for your growth needs (the top three levels of the pyramid) to come into play. Here's your opportunity to become motivated to reach your very greatest potential. Here's your chance at becoming financially literate.

GETTING STARTED ON YOUR FINANCIAL JOURNEY AND HOW TECHNOLOGY CAN HELP

As you will see in subsequent chapters in this book, technology is at the forefront of how we handle (but not necessarily successfully manage) our finances. Paychecks are automatically deposited. Debit cards take the place of carrying cash. Online bill payment is the monthly

Use technology to your advantage when it comes to managing your finances.

norm. Balances can be checked online from virtually any electronic device. It's quick. It's convenient. And it's easy. But "buyer beware."

Technology allows us to save time and headaches when tracking our funds. The only thing we seem to lose when using technology is the hands-on approach to our money—balancing our checkbook, getting cash to pay expenses, and the like (Jacobs, 2011). What often gets lost in all this technology is the ability to create and adhere to a budget, and that's where the trouble begins.

Each of the next five chapters in this book addresses the topics and skills you will need to lead you to becoming a financially literate person.

CASE IN POINT REVISITED

In the Case in Point presented at the beginning of this chapter, Lauren Bishop made the costly error of signing up for a credit card on campus and using it as soon as she received it. She allowed her desire for a new sweater to outweigh the financial burden its purchase would cost her, thus misinterpreting her needs from her wants.

Realizing after the first credit card statement came that she was in over her head financially, she decided to get an on-campus job two nights a week that would give her sufficient income to pay off her credit card as well as some extra money that she could use for the things she really wanted. She also decided to take the credit card out of her wallet and tuck it away in a drawer so she wouldn't be tempted to use it again.

CHAPTER SUMMARY

Chapter 1 introduced you to the concept of financial literacy. You are now familiar with what you need to do to be a financially literate individual and why being financially literate is important to your success. Conversely, you are aware of the challenges that can face an individual who is not financially literate.

POINTS TO KEEP IN MIND

- Financial literacy is the ability to use knowledge and skills to manage financial resources effectively for a lifetime of financial well-being.
- The financially literate person recognizes the pitfalls of poor financial management and seeks to avoid them.
- Identifying one's personal values helps clarify one's personal responsibilities when it comes to making financial decisions.
- It is important to distinguish between needs and wants.
- The use of technology can be of benefit when it comes to managing one's money.

CRITICAL THINKING QUESTIONS

1. What financial mistakes have you made at this stage in your life? How do you plan to correct them?

2. What are the advantages of "paying yourself first?"

3. From whom might you seek financial advice?

4. How do your personal goals affect your personal responsibilities when it comes to your finances?

5. How complete is your understanding of Maslow's hierarchy of needs? What level do you think you have reached on the pyramid? What changes can you make to reach the next level?

6. In what (desirable) ways might you express yourself aesthetically at home or in the classroom?

7. Do you use technology to your advantage when it comes to your finances? If so, how? In what areas might you improve?

8. Define *financial literacy*.

9. Name the specific knowledge required for an individual to be a financially literate student or professional.

10. Explain the importance of identifying one's personal values and personal responsibilities in terms of becoming financially literate.

11. Outline the challenges facing an individual who does not possess financial skills in school and in the workplace.

apply it!

 Activity #1: Self-Analysis: Grading Your Financial Acumen

GOAL: Critically assess where you stand in your "financial education" and generate a list of areas for improvement.

Using the following rating table, rate yourself in each area, using a scale from 1 to 4, where

　1 = what you know you don't know

　2 = what you think you might not know

　3 = what you think you know

　4 = what you know you know

　Be honest.

RATING TABLE	
Area	**Rating 1–4**
Creating, Adhering to, and Adjusting a Budget	
Saving While in College	
Saving for a Big Purchase	
Saving for Emergencies	
Saving for the Future	
Responsible Use of Credit Cards	
Good Debt Versus Bad Debt	
Avoiding Credit Card Fraud and Identity Theft	
Types of Bank Accounts and Banking Services	
How Online Banking Works	
Options for Financial Aid	
Getting and Paying Off Student Loans	
Obligations and Responsibilities for Paying Taxes	
Identifying Types of Taxes You Might Need to Pay	
Ways of Filing Taxes	
Consequences of Not Paying Taxes	

The remaining chapters in this book will address all the areas listed in the table.

Activity #2: Identifying Your Personal Values

GOAL: Identify your personal values and why these values are important to you.

STEP 1: Using the following table, identify the 10 personal values that are most important to you. A list of personal value examples has been provided for your use, or you may use your own.

MY PERSONAL VALUES	
Value	Why This Value is Important to Me

Personal value examples include the following:

Ambition, competency, individuality, equality, integrity, service, responsibility, accuracy, respect, dedication, diversity, improvement, enjoyment and fun, loyalty, credibility, honesty, innovativeness, teamwork, excellence, accountability, empowerment, quality, efficiency, dignity, collaboration, stewardship, empathy, accomplishment, courage, wisdom, independence, security, challenge, influence, learning, compassion, friendliness, discipline and order, generosity, persistency, optimism, dependability, flexibility

1

CHECK YOUR UNDERSTANDING

Visit www.cengagebrain.com to see how well you have mastered the material in Chapter 1.

REFERENCES

Bowman, M. (n.d.). *It's all about responsibility.* Retrieved October 20, 2011, from http://www.bowmansmoneycollege.com/Articles/Financial_responsibility.htm

Brunkhorst, S. (2005). *12 reflections on personal responsibility.* Retrieved November 3, 2011, from http://www.boxingscene.com/motivation/29761.php

CashCourse (2011[a]). *Accomplishing financial goals.* Retrieved October 26, 2011, from http://www.cashcourse.org/oregonstate//articles/id/1808/categoryid/113/accomplishing-financial-goals

CashCourse (2011[b]). *Defining financial goals.* Retrieved October 26, 2011, from http://www.cashcourse.org/oregonstate//articles/id/1807/categoryid/113/defining-financial-goals

Cherry, K. (n.d.). *Hierarchy of needs. The five levels of Maslow's hierarchy of needs.* Retrieved October 20, 2011, from http://psychology.about.com/od/theoriesofpersonality/a/hierarchyneeds.htm

Department of the Treasury (2008). President's Advisory Council on Financial Literacy. *2008 annual report to the president.* Retrieved October 26, 2011, from http://www.jumpstart.org/assets/files/PACFL_ANNUAL_REPORT_1-16-09.pdf

Federal Deposit Insurance Corporation (Spring 2005). FDIC Consumer News. Special Guide for Young Adults. Retrieved October 26, 2011, from http://www.fdic.gov/consumers/consumer/news/cnspr05/spring_05_bw.pdf

Garman, E. and Forgue, R. (2010). *Personal Finance, 10th ed.* Mason, OH: South-Western Cengage Learning.

Hereford, Z. (n.d.). *Have a personal value system.* Retrieved October 20, 2011, from www.essentiallifeskills.net/personalvaluesystem.html

Jacobs, D. (2011). *Has technology killed our ability to manage our money?* Retrieved October 20, 2011, from http://moneyhealthcentral.com/has-technology-ended-the-family-budget/

Martin, D. and Joomis, K. (2007). *Building Teachers: A Constructivist Approach to Introducing Education,* Belmont, CA: Wadsworth. Retrieved November 4, 2011, from http://academic.cengage.com/resource_uploads/downloads/0495570540_162121.pdf

Schmansky, R. (2010). *Building your financial foundation: watch out for money complacency.* Retrieved October 26, 2011, from http://blog.fpaforfinancial-planning.org/2010/07/27/building-your-financial-foundation-watch-out-for-money-complacency/

Schmansky, R. (2010). *Unsure of what to do next? Know where you stand in your financial life cycle.* Retrieved October 21, 2011, from http://blog.fpaforfinancialplanning.org/2010/07/12/unsure-of-what-to-do-next-know-where-you-stand-in-your-financial-life-cycle/

Shorb, V. (n.d.). National Financial Educators Council. *Financial literacy and the revival of the American dream.* Retrieved October 26, 2011, from http://www.financialeducatorscouncil.org/pdf/bonus/financial_literacy.pdf

Tracy, B. (n.d.) *Taking personal responsibility.* Retrieved November 2, 2011, from http://www.successmethods.org/brian_tracy-a19.html

Answer key for Financial Aptitude Test on p. 8

1. False
2. False
3. True
4. False
5. True
6. False
7. False
8. True
9. False
10. True

CHAPTER OUTLINE

Budgeting

Saving While in College

Saving for a Big Purchase

Saving for Emergencies

Saving for the Future

Insuring What You Have

2

Learning How to Budget, Save Your Money, and Insure What You Have

THE BIG PICTURE

You now have an understanding of the importance of being financially literate. Chapter 2 addresses the first steps in this process—learning how to budget, save your money, and insure what you have.

LEARNING OBJECTIVES

By the end of this chapter, you will achieve the following objectives:

▶ Develop effective ways to create, adjust, and adhere to a personal budget.

▶ Identify ways to save while in college.

▶ Describe strategies for saving for a big purchase.

▶ Examine the need to save for emergencies.

▶ List ways to save for the future.

▶ Explain different types of insurance.

2

CHAPTER 2 CASE IN POINT

Drew Pierpoint is a physical therapist in St. Louis who recently graduated from a Midwestern university with a degree in sports medicine. Drew has a regular monthly income from his job and no really large bills except his student loans. Once he started working, Drew dutifully made up a monthly budget using an online program, but he has found that he always goes over his budget each month because of his love of spending. To this end, his credit card balances are increasing while his paycheck hasn't, and he can't make ends meet.

Imagine yourself to be in Drew's position. Thoughtfully and honestly answer the following questions:

▶ Do you have—and follow—a monthly budget?

▶ Do you use credit cards to balance your budget?

▶ If you have one, does your budget tie into your near- and long-term financial goals?

▶ Do you plan for occasional, nonmonthly expenditures that impact your existing budget?

▶ Do you assess and adjust your budget on a regular basis?

BUDGETING

Your financial success is largely a matter of choice, not a matter of chance. A budget is where you make and implement those choices. A budget is your plan for spending and saving. Budgeting forces you to consider what is important in your life, what things you want to own, how you want to live, what it will take to do that, and, in the bigger picture, what you want to achieve in life. The budgeting process gives you control over your finances, and it empowers you to achieve your financial goals while simultaneously (and successfully) confronting any unforeseen events. In other words, budgeting answers the question, "What is my spending and savings action plan?" (Garman and Forgue, 2010).

A **budget** is a paper or electronic document used to record both planned and actual income and expenditures over a period of time. A budget helps you pay your bills on time and cover any unexpected expenses. It is a tool you should use faithfully to achieve your near- and long-term goals. As you work to create, adjust, and adhere to your budget, you should keep the following items in mind:

▶ **KEEP IT SIMPLE.** Budgets do not need to be complicated. You can use simple pencil and paper, a spreadsheet, or any sort of online budget worksheet or budget calculator tool. They are free and easy to use. (Visit www.cengagebrain.com for budget worksheets and budget calculator tools.) Use whatever technique works the best for you and one that you will continue to use because you are comfortable with it. The important thing is that you take the time to sit down and create a budget as a starting point. You can always (and should, on an as-needed basis) adjust your budget as your financial circumstances change.

▶ **MAKE IT PERSONAL.** As you have already learned, your financial goals are a direct outcome of your personal values. You will not meet your financial goals if they do not have significant meaning and value to you as an individual. If one of your goals is to purchase a home because that represents your personal value of security, then you need to make whatever financial adjustments are necessary to save up enough for a down payment within the time frame you have designated.

▶ **KEEP IT FLEXIBLE.** A budget is not set in stone. It is a working document that may need tweaks from time to time as your financial situation changes (all for the better, of course!). That does not mean, however, that you should change your budget on a monthly basis to accommodate your wants versus your needs. Be realistic about how you set up your budget but flexible in its use.

▶ **BE POSITIVE.** Don't think of a budget as a punishment because it's not. It's a proven, sound tool designed to help you stay financially ahead of the game, achieve your financial goals, and help you on your way to financial literacy.

Learning how to create a budget—and adhere to it—is one of the smartest financial moves you can make.

success steps for budgeting

- Keep It Simple
- Make It Personal
- Keep It Flexible
- Be Positive

CREATING A BUDGET

So how do you go about creating a budget? Fortunately, you already have most of the information you need. You know how much your rent, car payments, utilities, and the like are, so there's a good start. And you know the sources and amounts of your monthly income. What you may not know, however, is where else your money is going aside from the categories listed. Here are ways to create a budget from the ground up:

▶ **RECORD YOUR EXPENSES FOR A MONTH.** The best place to start the budgeting process is to save your receipts and record every transaction you make in a Word document, spreadsheet, notebook, or using another method, for a full month. Write down *everything* you purchase, from those morning lattes to ATM withdrawals to vending-machine drinks and snacks. You need to categorize these expenses to make the information meaningful. So, for example, track any food purchases (including eating out) that are not a part of a trip to the grocery store. Be sure to be specific with your information. If you went to Walmart and spent twenty-five dollars, don't just record "Spent $25 at Walmart." What did you spend that money on—socks, vitamins, dog food? Account for every item on that receipt.

At the end of a month's time, you should have a pretty good feel for where your money is going. You'll see purchasing patterns that can guide you to where you need to cut back and areas (only necessities, it is hoped) where you may need to allocate a bit more money each month.

▶ **RECORD INCOME AND NECESSARY EXPENSES.** Write down how much **net income** (income you receive after employer withholding for taxes and insurance) you bring home every month. Or, if you have a monthly allowance from the United Bank of Mom and Dad, use that figure instead.

Next, list the items you know you need to pay for during the course of a year. The exercise of recording 30 days of expenses will help you with this task. For bills that may fluctuate from month to month, such as electric and water bills, figure out the average amount over 12 months. If you have recently moved into a new place and do not have that history, call your utility company. They will have that information and can supply it to you.

Be sure to include expenses that come up once every six months or a year, such as insurance premiums and car registration renewal. And don't forget membership dues if you belong to any organizations. To account for these items on a monthly basis, divide the total amount by the term covered (say every six months), and include that in your monthly expenses.

Your final step is to subtract all of your expenses from your income. Are you lucky enough to be ahead of the game? If so, use that extra money (called **discretionary income**) to fuel your financial goals. These goals can include anything from establishing an emergency fund, to taking that vacation, to paying down debt, or to starting retirement savings (remember, it's never too early to start saving). However, if you are like most of us, your expenses will outweigh your income, and that's a disheartening feeling, to say the least.

ADJUSTING A BUDGET

After you've come to the realization that more money is going out than is coming in, the next step in the budget process is to make some budget adjustments. Some of your expenses are fixed, such as rent, a car payment, and insurance costs. But other expenses are considered flexible. These areas include (but are not limited to) entertainment, clothing, groceries, eating out, and the like. Take a close look at these areas to see where you can modify your allocated dollar amounts. Consider what in these flexible categories are needs and what are wants. You need groceries, but you want a latte every day. Making coffee at home every morning and eliminating the Starbucks stop can save you a significant amount of money in the long term—money that you can apply to the necessities.

When you are adjusting your budget, be realistic. Don't cut your grocery money in half when you barely have enough food around the house as it is. This may look good on paper, but your stomach will surely not appreciate it.

If you've made all the adjustments that you reasonably can and your expenses still outweigh your income, it may be time to consider other sources of revenue. Can you work extra hours at your current job, take on a second job, housesit? If you have a credit card, consider contacting the company to negotiate a lower payment. The bottom line is *don't spend more than you earn.*

ADHERING TO A BUDGET

So you now have a budget in place. Congratulations to you! Next, you must move into the final stage of budgeting, and that is to adhere to what you have created. Having a budget and ignoring it is like ignoring your health. At some point, something bad is going to happen. And you won't like it when it does.

Monitoring your spending and comparing it against your budget each month will keep your finances in check. If you've allocated $50 for entertainment and you've used that up by midmonth, don't spend any more on it until the following month. Period. It's easy to slip, of course, but reminding yourself of your budget every time you spend (especially in the wants category) will help you stay on track to fulfill your financial goals (Lynnae, 2008).

SAVING WHILE IN COLLEGE

The phrase "saving while in college" may seem like an oxymoron to the average college student. College students are notoriously perceived as being broke or barely making it from semester to semester. This is not the case for all college students, obviously, but it is a fact of life for many students on campus.

As disheartening as that may sound, and as much as this reality may ring true for you, there *are* ways to save money while in college. This saving exercise has two approaches:

- Open some sort of **savings account** and put money aside each month.

- Find ways to cut back on your expenses so that you are not broke or fall short all the time. Let's take a look at both approaches.

- **PUTTING MONEY ASIDE EACH MONTH.** If you are living on a limited/fixed amount of income from your parents, putting money away each month in a savings account may not be feasible. But, if you are working full- or part-time, you should strongly consider this choice. There are several options for savings accounts, but one of the most attractive ones to college students is a student savings account. Major banks all vie for student accounts, whether checking, savings, or other types of accounts, and they tend to offer freebies as an incentive to choose their bank over a competitor's. Some possible benefits banks may offer to entice you to their student savings account services include the following:

- No minimum balance
- No monthly fee
- Online banking
- Competitive interest rates
- Available overdraft protection (fees often apply, however)
- Automatic transfers from your checking to your college savings account
- Easy transfers from parents' accounts to student savings accounts

As with any banking service, it's wise to shop around to get the best deal and find a program that best suits your needs. If you already have a checking account at a financial institution, start there first. If nothing else, it will be a cinch to move funds from your checking account into your savings account automatically or through online banking services. Be sure to compare competitive interest rates among banks so that you will realize the greatest return on your money. It also doesn't hurt to keep tabs on your bank's competitors' interest rates, which, after a time, may be better than what you are currently getting on your account. Just be sure that you weigh the benefits that each bank offers and to read the fine print to determine if there are any hidden costs or penalties.

▶ **CUTTING BACK ON EXPENSES.** This is easier said than done, of course. Many expenses are fixed, such as rent, car payments, insurance, and the like. If you have been diligent about tracking your expenses and creating a budget, you have identified the monies you absolutely need each month to make those payments. However, there are several flexible expense areas where you can make reasonable adjustments to cut back without really compromising your lifestyle. In fact, making some of these suggested adjustments can actually ease your stress levels because you are not sweating it out each month or semester.

2

Remember the needs versus wants discussion from earlier in this book. Downgrading a want to a need will still achieve a desired result at less cost and with greater financial satisfaction. This is financial literacy personified.

Here are three major areas where you can make changes immediately that will positively affect your bottom line. This list is hardly exhaustive, but these areas generally impact college students the most and are among the easiest to change if you do not let peer pressure get the best of you. These areas include the following:

▶ **FOOD.** If you are on a meal plan, whether living on campus or not, use it to the fullest extent. It's been paid for, and if you don't use all the allotted meals, then you are throwing money away. Conversely, if you have gone through all your meals on a weekly basis and still need to supplement eating outside the plan, then you are routinely spending out-of-pocket money that you likely hadn't anticipated (nor budgeted). Evaluate your use of the plan prior to signing up for next semester's plan and adjust it accordingly.

Even if your meal plan is sufficient for your needs, the lure of pizza delivery, snacking at the student union, or the fast-food drive-through window is palpable. Peer pressure to participate in impromptu food activities can also be a mighty pull when you know better. Sure, it's perfectly acceptable (and comforting) to have the occasional take out or delivery, but making this action into a habit will wreak havoc on your wallet.

If you live in a dorm, one way to supplement your meal plan and to fuel your late-night study time is to stock up on nutritional snacks and drinks. Virtually all students have access to a refrigerator, either in their own room or in a common area, so take advantage of it. Stock items such as yogurt, string cheese, and cottage cheese, making sure you keep an eye on expiration dates. Store nonperishable items such as granola bars, bagels, and peanut butter in your room, and tap into those items when the munchies hit. If you (and perhaps a roommate or other friend) go to the grocery store even once a month to stock up on items, you will eat more nutritious food and save money at a really good pace. And just say no to the vending and soda machines in the lobby!

2

If you live in an apartment or off-campus housing, you have a distinct budgetary advantage: a kitchen. Even if it is small, a kitchen opens up a whole world to you. You need not be a gourmet cook or have myriad appliances to feed yourself (and perhaps a roommate or two) well on a consistent basis. If you're new to cooking and need ideas, literally hundreds of thousands of recipes are available online. The important thing is to keep staples around so that you can pull together even a simple meal every day. Here are some cost-saving ideas for when you grocery shop:

- **Go grocery shopping on a full stomach.** If you're hungry, it's harder to concentrate and you'll be more apt to buy things you hadn't planned on (or budgeted).

- **Always go with a list, and stick to it.** You will spend less on food if you shop with a list. It's amazing how quickly those impulse items can ruin your well-intentioned shopping plans.

- **Limit the number of trips to the store each month.** Try to keep your pantry stocked with the basics (which you should always buy on sale, if possible), and then fill in once every two weeks or so with perishable items. Frequent trips to the store for just a few things can be killer on your wallet.

- **Get a local grocery store saver card.** Grocery chains are highly competitive and their profit margins are remarkably slim. Because of this, stores like to reward their customers for their loyalty by giving discounts on items when the card is used. You can also register at the chain's web site and download digital coupons directly to your card. When you purchase an item that has a coupon loaded on the card, you will receive the discounted price after you swipe your card at the checkout.

- **Cut coupons and check store sales flyers.** Despite our ever-growing online environment, 80 percent of all coupons *still* come from the Sunday paper. It is worth a dollar or two and a bit of your time each week to get the Sunday paper and cut out the coupons for items that you need. Couple that with weekly sales flyers and you can rack up substantial savings. Check your receipts to see how you

2

are doing—your amount of savings will be indicated on the bottom. One note of caution, however. Do not buy a brand-name item simply because you have a coupon and can save a little coin. Store-brand items are always less expensive and the quality is often as good as the national brand names.

- **Purchase basic ingredients.** Keep household staples on hand at all times. Items like flour, sugar, rice, potatoes, and various canned and frozen goods will allow you to whip up a meal in no time. Avoid convenience foods if at all possible. Prepackaged components or ready-made items cost appreciably more because you are paying a premium for somebody else doing the work. Plus, most of these items are full of processed ingredients that do not help your heart, your cholesterol, or your waistline.

▶ **TRANSPORTATION.** If you are living on campus, then using your feet, a bicycle, or perhaps a campus shuttle is the norm for you. But if you commute to class or live off campus, then here are some cost-saving options that you might consider:

- **Use public transportation.** Sure, it can be a headache to use it sometimes, but your city provides it because it's relatively inexpensive, it gets you where you need to go, and it cuts down on congestion and pollution. Be sure to check for monthly passes or student passes that offer substantial discounts.

- **Limit the use of your car.** If you do own a car, owner beware. Not only are cars expensive to purchase, they can be a money pit to use and maintain. Consider your costs when it comes to gas, parking, insurance, maintenance, and car payments. Investigate carpooling some days of the week and maybe using public transportation other days of the week instead of driving to work or class each day. Most metropolitan areas have some sort of carpooling program. Your city or state's official web site will have the details on how you can take advantage of this service. Many campuses also offer a ride-share program at no cost. Check with your Student Services office (or your school's intranet site) for information about how the program works.

2

- **Keep your vehicle in top shape.** Sometimes circumstances do not allow you to use public transportation, walk, or carpool. If that is the case and you must drive (whether to campus or to a job), then make a habit of keeping your car in the best shape possible.

▶ **ENTERTAINMENT.** Entertainment is one of the categories that can render you penniless without much effort. So many items come under this umbrella that you may not even realize they are wants instead of needs. For example, do you have cable TV? If so, how much do you pay each month for that service? And what about those premium channels (HBO, Showtime, Cinemax, and the like)? If you've subscribed to any of those, your monthly costs are even higher.

Some entertainment costs are obvious. Attending movies, concerts, and eating out are three of the most common areas where college students spend money. Other entertainment costs may not be as noticeable—items such as iTunes downloads, gamer subscriptions, video games, CDs, and renting movies all contribute to how much you have left over for the necessities (Caldwell, n.d. [a]). If you are putting your entertainment needs above what you really need, then you are breaking one of the tenets of being financially literate.

All is not lost, however. No one is saying that you shouldn't have fun and be entertained. Here are some ways to cut back on your entertainment costs and still have a great time:

- **Use your computer as both a television and a stereo.** If you already have access to cable (and the cost is not prohibitive), don't go to the expense of buying a TV. Use the DVD/CD player in your computer to listen to music and watch movies. If you don't have cable, you can still stream many live events (such as sporting events) to stay current.

- **Rethink going to the movies.** Do you have to see the latest blockbuster as soon as it comes out? Consider going to a matinee instead of an evening show. Prices are lower during the day, and you'll get greater mileage out of your student discount card this way. Also, check campus postings for free movies on campus. There's a good chance that you can see classics, independents, student films, and film noir at no cost.

2

- **Rent; don't buy.** Rent DVDs as a group. Pass the disc along to your responsible friends before the due date. Everyone gets to watch at a fraction of the cost to rent individually. Subscribing to a DVD rental service is also a cost-savings measure. There is more and more competition out there in this arena, so comparison shop before you subscribe.

- **Take advantage of free local and campus events.** Many communities support free events such as concerts, arts and crafts fairs, indoor-outdoor theater, festivals, and free days at art galleries and museums. The vast majority of campuses also provide free or low-cost entertainment, especially on weekends (Collegescholarships.org, n.d.).

---

success steps for saving while in college

- Open some type of savings account.
- Cut back on expenses.
  - Food
    - Go grocery shopping on a full stomach.
    - Always go with a list and stick to it.
    - Limit the number of trips to the store each month.
    - Get a local grocery store saver card.
    - Cut coupons and use store sales flyers.
    - Purchase basic ingredients.
  - Transportation
    - Use public transportation.
    - Limit the use of your car.
    - Keep your vehicle in top shape.
  - Entertainment
    - Use your computer as both a television and a stereo.
    - Rethink going to the movies.
    - Rent; don't buy.
    - Take advantage of free local and campus events.

SAVING FOR A BIG PURCHASE

At some point in your life (and maybe you are already there), you will consider making a big purchase. The definition of a big purchase can vary greatly from individual to individual both in terms of dollar amount and necessity, but when it is time for you to make such a purchase, you should follow some basic guidelines:

The federal government's General Services Administration (GSA) publishes the *Consumer Action Handbook* annually and offers helpful advice for anyone considering a major purchase:

▶ Decide in advance exactly what you want and what you can afford.

▶ Do your research. Ask family, friends, and others you trust for advice based on their experience.

▶ Gather information about the seller and the item or service you are purchasing.

▶ Review product test results and other information from consumer experts.

▶ Get advice and price quotes from several sellers.

▶ Check out a company's complaint record with your local consumer affairs office and Better Business Bureau.

Yuri Arcurs/Shutterstock.com

Take the time to fully research all aspects of making a big purchase, including deciding what you really can afford.

2

▶ Get a written copy of guarantees and warranties.

▶ Get the seller's refund, return, and cancellation policies.

▶ Ask whom to contact if you have a question or problem.

▶ Read and understand any contract or legal document you are asked to sign. Make sure the contract has no blank spaces. Insist that any extras you are promised be put in writing.

▶ Consider paying by credit card. If you have a problem, you can dispute a charge made on your credit card (but don't use this as an excuse to use your credit card).

▶ Don't buy on impulse or under pressure. This includes donating to charity (U.S. General Services Administration, 2011).

The preceding list may seem exhaustive and unnecessary, but it really is the best idea if you do your homework in advance of making that big purchase. The more you research and plan, the better off you will be (and happier, too, because you know you made an informed purchasing decision). You really need to take all of these items into consideration, but the most important one is listed first: *Decide in advance exactly what you want and what you can afford.*

Bear in mind that what you want and what you can afford are two separate issues. You may *want* that 42-inch 1080p 120Hz LED-LCD HDTV (especially in time for the *big* game), but the stark reality is that you do not currently have the funds to pay for it outright. You simply can't afford it right now. Because you are becoming financially literate, you realize that using your credit card is not the right way to go. Good for you!

Here are some suggestions for planning and saving for a big purchase, whether it is that TV, a new or used car, or a home:

▶ **DO THE MATH.** Determine how much you need to save, and for how many months. Don't forget to account for any taxes, shipping and handling or delivery fees, insurance, extended warranties, or other charges that may be associated with your purchase when making your calculation. (Visit www.cengagebrain.com for an online calculator that will help you with your figuring.)

▶ **DECIDE WHERE TO SAVE YOUR MONEY.** If you already have a savings account, that's a logical place to put your monthly

2

contribution. Another option is to open a money market account or certificate of deposit (CD). Both of these types of accounts let you withdraw money only at set times. In return, you'll earn a higher interest rate than a standard savings account. This might be an excellent choice because you can't be tempted to use that money freehand for something else. Check with your financial institution to see what might be the best alternative, keeping in mind any fees the bank may charge (smartaboutmoney.org, n.d. [a]).

▶ **CONSIDER USING LAYAWAY.** If your store has a layaway policy, investigate the rules and determine how many weeks the policy covers. Some stores allow layaway only near the holidays; other stores have a year-round policy. If you go this route, keep track of the terms of the contract, all receipts, and all payments that you have made (smartaboutmoney.org, n.d. [b]).

▶ **BRING IN THE EXPERTS.** You may not need much advice when it comes to purchasing that TV, but you should seek wise counsel from the experts if you are saving to purchase a new or used car or a home. Your financial institution, finance company (whether for a house or a car), or mortgage company have people who are schooled in the best choices for you, given your purchasing circumstances. Sure, each company you contact wants your business, but it is best if you listen to what these companies have to say and do some comparison shopping. In this way, you will know all the financial obligations you will likely encounter and can adjust your savings plan accordingly.

---

success steps for saving for a big purchase

- Do the math.
- Decide where to save your money.
- Consider using layaway.
- Bring in the experts.

SAVING FOR EMERGENCIES

No one plans for emergencies. They just happen. Emergencies that can cause you financial distress range from job loss to car or house repairs to significant medical expenses or something that you've never even imagined.

You can't control the emergencies that find you, but you can control how you handle those emergencies from a financial standpoint. Conventional wisdom says that you should have anywhere from three to six months of net income tucked away to be used when any emergency arises (which, sadly, is most commonly job loss). Depending on your circumstances, this may represent a significant amount of ready cash. If you are living paycheck to paycheck, you likely cannot fathom putting anything away for that rainy day.

The advice that experts tend to give is to start small but to start regardless. Even if you can tuck away only $10 a week for a few weeks, at least you are working on building up an emergency war chest that you can tap into when the need arises. As your financial situation improves, improve your emergency fund as well. Increase the amount you save as soon as you can. If you have to tap into that fund and deplete it, start saving money again because something else will always come along.

As with other savings ideas discussed in this chapter, do some research to decide what emergency savings vehicle is right for you. Just remember that you want your money to be fluid, as in easy to access, so do not consider investing those funds (where you can lose money) or putting them into a CD that has restrictions on when you can make a withdrawal. The financially literate person recognizes that emergencies are inevitable and that saving for them is important.

SAVING FOR THE FUTURE

By now you are probably thinking, "It's already been suggested that I save money while I am in college, save money for a big purchase, and save money for emergencies. Just how am I supposed to save money for the future as well?"

As daunting and perhaps unrealistic as it may seem, if you follow the suggestions in this book, you are well on your way to saving for the future. Here's why:

It is never too early to start saving for the "good life" and financial freedom.

▶ **YOU'VE IDENTIFIED YOUR FINANCIAL GOALS.** By doing so, you have entwined your personal values with what you want your money to accomplish for you in your lifetime. In this way, you realize that certain financial scenarios must play out for that to happen.

▶ **YOU KNOW YOUR CURRENT FINANCIAL SITUATION.** By creating and adhering to a budget, you can account for not only how much money you have but also where it goes each month. When you go over your budget, you know enough to adjust it and cut back in some areas so that you do make ends meet and can still live a happy life and have some fun.

▶ **YOU RECOGNIZE VARYING WAYS TO SAVE MONEY.** As you become more financially literate, you become aware of more ways to keep yourself financially balanced *and* diligent about saving even a small amount of money, including paying yourself first. You understand that cost-savings measures while in school can lead to saving for a big purchase, and you have the tools for how to go about that intelligently. You also realize that emergencies will happen and that being able to react to those emergencies in a financially responsible way is the proper course of action.

RETIREMENT PLANNING

For many (if not most) of us, saving for the future entails being able to retire at some point in our lives. **Retirement** may seem light years away if you are still in school and have barely or never entered the workforce. But that reality will be here sooner rather than later, so it truly is not too early to think about, and put into motion, ways that you can save for your golden years.

To be financially secure in your retirement, you must plan for it, commit to that plan, and use your money wisely. The U.S.

2

Department of Labor cites the following statistics as they relate to retirement:

▶ Fewer than half of Americans have calculated how much they need to save for retirement.

▶ In 2009, 13 percent of private industry workers with access to a defined **contribution plan**, such as a 401(k), did not participate. A contribution plan is an employer-sponsored retirement plan that accepts employee as well as employer contributions.

▶ The average American spends 20 years in retirement (United States Department of Labor 2010).

Don't be a part of these statistics! Consider the following retirement tips as you enter your postgraduate years:

▶ **MAKE SAVING FOR RETIREMENT A PRIORITY.** Devise a plan, stick to it, and set goals. Remember, it's never too early or too late to start saving.

▶ **KNOW YOUR RETIREMENT NEEDS.** Retirement is expensive. Experts estimate that you will need about 70 percent of your preretirement income to maintain your standard of living when you stop working.

▶ **CONTRIBUTE TO YOUR EMPLOYER'S RETIREMENT SAVINGS PLAN.** If your employer offers a retirement savings plan, such as a **401(k) plan**, sign up and contribute all you can. Your taxes will be lower, your company may kick in more (called a **matching contribution**), and automatic payroll deductions make it easy. Over time, compound interest and **tax deferrals** make a big difference in the amount you will accumulate.

▶ **LEARN ABOUT YOUR EMPLOYER'S PENSION PLAN.** If your employer has a traditional **pension** plan, check to see if you are covered by the plan and learn how it works.

▶ **CONSIDER BASIC INVESTMENT PRINCIPLES.** How you save can be as important as how much you save. **Inflation** and the types of **investments** you make play important roles in how much you will have saved at retirement.

▶ **DON'T TOUCH YOUR RETIREMENT SAVINGS.** If you withdraw your retirement savings now, you'll lose **principal** and **interest**, and you may lose tax benefits or have to pay withdrawal penalties. If you change jobs, leave your savings invested in your current retirement plan, or roll them over to an **Individual Retirement Account (IRA)** or your new employer's plan.

▶ **PUT MONEY INTO AN INDIVIDUAL RETIREMENT ACCOUNT.** You can put up to $5,000 a year into an Individual Retirement Account (IRA); you can contribute even more if you are 50 or older. You can also start with much less. IRAs also provide tax advantages and can provide an easy way to save. You can set it up so that an amount is automatically deducted from your checking or savings account and deposited in the IRA.

▶ **FIND OUT ABOUT YOUR SOCIAL SECURITY BENEFITS.** Social Security pays benefits that are on average 40 percent of what you earned before retirement. You should receive a **Social Security Statement** each year that gives you an estimate of how much your benefit will be and when you can receive it.

▶ **ASK QUESTIONS.** While these tips are meant to point you in the right direction, you'll need more information. Talk to your employer, your bank, your union, or a financial advisor. Ask questions and make sure you understand the answers. Get practical advice and act now (United States Department of Labor, 2010).

success steps for retirement planning

- Make saving for retirement a priority.
- Know your retirement needs.
- Contribute to your employer's retirement savings plan.
- Learn about your employer's pension plan.
- Consider basic investment principles.
- Don't touch your retirement savings.
- Put money into an Individual Retirement Account.
- Find out about your Social Security benefits.
- Ask questions.

2

INSURING WHAT YOU HAVE

So far in your life, you may not have considered the need for various types of insurance. If you've been living at home, your parents have most likely provided the proper coverage (health insurance, for example), except maybe for car insurance if you own a car and they have made that your responsibility.

Although it is yet another expense, basic insurance coverage is essential. Basic insurance is a mechanism that protects your assets and finances from accidents, illness, theft, and other financially damaging situations. Now that you are working toward your financial independence and are taking on a greater decision-making role in your life, you need to be aware of not only the minimal types of insurance you should carry but also the types of insurance mistakes you should avoid. These include the following:

▶ **NOT HAVING BASIC INSURANCE.** Do not file this notion as a way to save money. You won't. Not having insurance will cost you way more in the end than paying monthly premiums.

▶ **OVERINSURING YOURSELF.** At this stage in your life, you may not have many assets, so do not pay for more coverage than you need. An independent insurance agent can help you with this process.

▶ **UNDERINSURING YOURSELF.** Likewise, underinsuring yourself can lead to financial disaster. Know what dollar amounts your policies will pay out and make sure those payouts will sufficiently cover your expenses.

▶ **GETTING THE WRONG INSURANCE.** At this stage of your life, you do not need every conceivable type of coverage available. Get the policies that apply to your life situation, and leave it at that.

▶ **NOT SHOPPING AROUND.** Before you purchase any type of insurance, shop around, just like you would for any major purchase. Many insurance companies offer discounts for multiple policies. Also, be sure to revisit all of your policies every couple of years to find the most competitive rates at the time (Caldwell, n.d. [b]).

TYPES OF INSURANCE POLICIES YOU NEED

Auto Insurance

If you own a car, having car insurance is mandatory. In fact, most states require that you have basic car insurance. Your car may be your most expensive asset at the moment, so be sure that you have adequate coverage to replace its value. Many types of insurance options fall under the general umbrella of car insurance, so be sure to shop around to get the best deal on the type of coverage you need. Also, be sure to check into any discounts offered for such items as your age, good grades if you are still in school, and your driving record.

Health Insurance

Without a doubt, you need health insurance. Health costs are skyrocketing, and the costs of even a minor illness or accident can send your finances reeling. If you are still in school, you should be covered by your parents' policy. Also check into how long you are covered, even if you have graduated and entered the workforce. If you are working, your employer most likely offers some sort of health coverage at a discounted rate to its employees. If you have no other options, then pay for coverage that has a high deductible so the monthly premium is lower.

Property Insurance

If you own a home, you are required to have homeowner's insurance. The bank or mortgage company that holds your loan (mortgage) requires that the asset be adequately insured. Generally, the insurance premium is built into the monthly payment.

If you rent a home or an apartment, renter's insurance is equally important. Renter's insurance does not cover the actual structure; the owner of the building is required to have that coverage. What renter's insurance does cover are your belongings in the event of a fire, theft, or other mishap. You should have a policy that can cover most of your replacement costs.

Life Insurance

Life insurance is generally not thought of as being necessary at a young age. It becomes more important to have a policy if you are married and/or have children. If you are employed, check with your employer to see if they offer basic coverage as a benefit (Caldwell, n.d. [c]).

2

CASE IN POINT REVISITED

In the Case in Point presented at the beginning of this chapter, Drew Pierpoint came up with a monthly budget after he graduated from school and started a job as a physical therapist. While Drew's budget did capture his monthly expenses, he could not adhere to it because of his love of spending.

Tired of mounting credit card debt and realizing that having a budget but not following it was a sham, Drew found ways to cut back on his entertainment and food expenses. He also took it to heart that he could not go over budgeted amounts. After a few months, Drew was able to meet his budget, pay down his credit cards, and start saving for his future plans.

CHAPTER SUMMARY

Chapter 2 introduced you to the concepts of budgeting, how to save money, and how to insure what you have. You learned that budgeting is a three-part process: creating, adjusting, and adhering to it. You also learned the importance of saving money and identified many ways to save to meet a variety of financial goals, now and in the future. Finally, you recognized the importance of having basic insurance policies to protect yourself, your loved ones, and your assets.

POINTS TO KEEP IN MIND

- Budgeting is an important financial tool that guides you toward financial literacy.
- A budget is a working document that may be adjusted if it isn't working for you.
- Once set, you must stick to your budget for it to be effective.
- There are many ways to save money while in college, most notably in the areas of food, transportation, and entertainment.

▶ Saving for a big purchase can be accomplished by doing research ahead of the purchase, deciding where and how to save the money for that purchase, and bringing in expert advice when necessary.

▶ Saving for emergencies is a necessary action for the financially literate person.

▶ Saving for the future is primarily about planning for one's retirement.

▶ Having the right types of insurance policies will protect your assets, your health, and your loved ones.

CRITICAL THINKING QUESTIONS

1. How does using a budget impact what you want to achieve in life financially?

2. Besides food, transportation, and entertainment, in what other areas can you save money while in college?

3. How do you determine if a big purchase fits into your financial goals?

4. What might be some immediate and long-term financial ramifications if you have an emergency?

5. Would the absence of health or other insurance benefits impact your decision whether to take a job or not?

apply it!

 Activity #1: Budget Worksheet/Calculator

GOAL: Develop an awareness of the types of budget worksheets and calculators available on the Internet.

STEP 1: Using a search engine, type the words *budget worksheet*. Click on several of the results and do a comparison. Choose a worksheet that best fits your needs and save it to your hard drive.

STEP 2: Using a search engine, type the words *budget calculator*. Click on several of the results and do a comparison. Choose a calculator that best fits your needs and save it to your hard drive.

STEP 3: Use both the chosen budget worksheet and chosen budget calculator to create a budget. Decide on your preference for use and continue to use that method for creating and adjusting your monthly budget.

 Activity #2: Saving Money While in College

GOAL: Emphasize the importance of saving money while in college.

STEP 1: As a group, brainstorm answers to the following questions. Use your imagination. Think critically and creatively. Remember that in brainstorming, the goal is to generate as many ideas as possible but not to judge or evaluate those ideas.

- Where can I save money on campus?
- How can I save money on clothing?
- How can I save money on books?
- How can I save money on computer hardware and software?

STEP 2: Be prepared to compare your list with those of other groups in your class.

CHECK YOUR UNDERSTANDING

 Visit www.cengagebrain.com to see how well you have mastered the material in Chapter 2.

2

REFERENCES

Caldwell, M. (n.d. [a]). *How to trim 3 common budget categories.* Retrieved December 5, 2011, from http://moneyfor20s.about.com/od/budgeting/a/trimbudgetcat.htm

Caldwell, M. (n.d. [b]). *5 basic insurance mistakes to avoid.* Retrieved December 7, 2011, from http://moneyfor20s.about.com/od/protectingyourself/tp/common-insurance-mistakes.htm

Caldwell, M. (n.d. [c]). *Types of insurance policies you need.* Retrieved December 7, 2011, from http://financialplan.about.com/od/insurance/a/insuredoneed.htm

Collegescholarships.org (n.d.). *118 ways to save money in college.* Retrieved December 5, 2011, from http://www.collegescholarships.org/student-living/save-money.htm

Garman, E. and Forgue, R. (2010). *Personal Finance (10th ed.).* Mason, OH: South-Western Cengage Learning.

Lynnae (2008). *How to make a budget that works.* Retrieved November 10, 2011, from http://beingfrugal.net/2008/03/03/how-to-make-a-budget/

Smartaboutmoney.org (n.d. [a]). *Big ticket items.* Retrieved December 7, 2011, from http://www.smartaboutmoney.org/LifeEventsFinancialDecisions/PlanningaMajorPurchase/BigTicketItems/tabid/354/Default.aspx

Smartaboutmoney.org (n.d. [b]). *Is layaway right for you?* Retrieved December 8, 2011, from http://www.smartaboutmoney.org/FeaturedArticles/IsLayawayRightForYou/tabid/774/Default.aspx

U.S. General Services Administration (2011). *2011 Consumer Action Handbook.* Retrieved December 7, 2011, from http://publications.usa.gov/USAPubs.php?PubID=5131

United States Department of Labor (2011). *Top 10 ways to prepare for retirement.* Retrieved December 13, 2011, from http://www.dol.gov/ebsa/publications/10_ways_to_prepare.html

wongwean/Shutterstock.com

CHAPTER OUTLINE

Positive Financial Behaviors versus Risky Credit Behaviors

Good Debt versus Bad Debt

Benefits and Dangers of Owning a Credit Card

Credit Card Fraud and Identity Theft

3

Personal Credit Cards: Good or Bad?

LEARNING OBJECTIVES

By the end of this chapter, you will achieve the following objectives:

▶ Distinguish between positive financial behaviors and risky credit behaviors.

▶ Compare good debt versus bad debt.

▶ Identify how credit cards can affect your financial well-being.

▶ Know the laws that govern the use of credit cards.

▶ Describe issues surrounding credit card fraud and identity theft.

THE BIG PICTURE

While there are many benefits to owning a credit card, such as establishing a good credit rating, real and potentially long-lasting negative consequences can result from mismanaging this personal financial tool. Chapter 3 identifies ways to use credit cards to your financial advantage.

3

CHAPTER 3 CASE IN POINT

Hailey Mann is a registered dietician who is in the market for a new car. Despite a trade-in, a down payment, and a dealership rebate, she knows that she will have to take out a loan to cover the remaining cost of the purchase. She hasn't saved any additional funds; she has only the down payment. Hailey anticipates getting the car loan through the dealership and did not plan on talking to her financial institution prior to the purchase.

Hailey found a car that met her needs and was well within her price range. When it came time to negotiate the car's financing, she filled out the various required forms and waited to hear from the dealership as to when she could close the deal. A few days later, the dealership's salesman called to say that her loan request had been denied because her credit score was 600 and her credit report had some recent negative entries.

Imagine yourself to be in Hailey's position. Thoughtfully and honestly answer the following questions:

▶ Do you pay your bills on time?

▶ Do you know your credit score?

▶ How long is your credit history?

▶ Do you know what it says in your credit report?

▶ Have you applied for new credit recently?

▶ How many and what types of credit accounts do you have?

POSITIVE FINANCIAL BEHAVIORS VERSUS RISKY CREDIT BEHAVIORS

Being out on your own can be fun and exciting, but it also means taking on new financial responsibilities. The decisions you make now about how you manage your finances and borrow money will affect you in the future—for better or worse.

Did you know that there are companies that keep track of whether you pay your debts and if you make payments on time?

Marie C Fields/Shutterstock.com

Having too many credit cards puts you at immediate financial risk.

These companies then make this information available in the form of a credit report and credit score.

A bad credit history can haunt you for a long time—seven years or more. That's why the best thing to do is learn how to maintain good credit before a problem occurs. This might seem complicated at first, but it gets easier once you understand the basics of credit and how it works.

Credit is more than just a plastic card you use to buy things—it is your financial trustworthiness. Good credit means that your history of payments, employment, and salary make you a good candidate for a loan, and **creditors**—those who lend money or services—will be more willing to work with you. Having good credit usually translates into lower payments and more ease in borrowing money. Bad credit, however, can be a big problem. It usually results from making payments late or borrowing too much money, and it means that you might have trouble getting a car loan, a credit card, a place to live and, sometimes, a job (Federal Trade Commission, 2009).

If you do decide to have one or more credit cards, it is in your financial best interest to handle them responsibly. Demonstrating positive financial behaviors goes a long way toward securing your

3

financial future and meeting the long-term goals that are important to you. These behaviors include the following:

▶ **USING A BUDGET.** As you have already learned, creating and adhering to a budget is perhaps the most important habit you can adopt to keep yourself on track financially.

▶ **SAVING REGULARLY.** This goes hand in hand with the use of a budget. And, as it has been noted, it's never too early to start saving.

▶ **USING CREDIT RESPONSIBLY.** You learn a great deal more about this later in this chapter. Continual responsible credit use will keep you out of financial trouble now and into the future.

Risky credit behaviors jeopardize good credit. Risky credit behaviors are very easy to fall into and hard to climb out of. Financial shortfalls oftentimes make us panic about meeting our financial obligations, and the ever-present lure of wants can call out to us at any time. Risky credit behaviors include (but are not limited to) the following:

▶ **MAXING OUT YOUR CREDIT CARD(S).** All credit cards come with spending (credit) limits. If you charge up to your limit amount, or worse, go over it, you are subjecting yourself to two problems. One, your card issuer will charge you a penalty, which is expensive (typically $30 for each instance). Two, if you exceed your credit limit, you may damage your credit score, which may translate into higher interest rates, both now and in the future (Federal Deposit Insurance Corporation, 2007).

▶ **MAKING LATE PAYMENTS.** Don't wait until the last minute to pay your monthly bills. Paying your bills on time helps you maintain a good credit record and allows you to qualify for low interest rates. Consumers who pay their credit card bills late may face a major hike in their interest rate—often between 29 and 35 percent. Late payments on these cards can trigger rate increases on other cards or loans, especially if your credit record shows other signs of risk. And don't forget that credit card companies love to charge fees whenever and wherever they can. Late-payment fees of $30 or more show up on your credit card statement the month after you are late, which means you'll be paying interest on that added amount (Federal Deposit Insurance Corporation, 2007).

▶ **NEGLECTING TO PAY OFF YOUR CREDIT CARD BALANCE EACH MONTH.** It may not be easy, but if possible, pay your bill in full each month. Paying only the minimum due each month means you'll be paying a lot of interest for many years, and those costs could far exceed the amount of your original purchase (Federal Deposit Insurance Corporation, 2005).

GOOD DEBT VERSUS BAD DEBT

So far in this book, you have seen examples of unwise spending habits, the failure to devise and use a budget, the consequences of not saving money, and risky credit behaviors. All of these poor financial patterns can lead, in some fashion, to the opportunity for an individual to accumulate an overwhelming amount of debt.

According to CNNMoney, "Ideally, your total long-term debt payments, including your mortgage and credit cards, should not exceed 36 percent of your gross monthly income." However, when this ideal debt payment scenario is not met, people turn to the quick-and-easy fix of using credit cards to meet their obligations. CardWeb.com, an online publisher of information about the payments industry (companies that offer credit cards, debit cards, prepaid cards, ATM cards, loyalty cards, and the like), states that the average U.S. household with at least one credit card carries a balance of just under $11,000! Avoiding debt altogether is a lofty goal, but not if it means depleting all of your savings and investments for emergencies. The trick is to determine which debt makes sense, which does not, and then effectively manage the money you do borrow (CNNMoney, n.d. [b]).

In essence, there are two types of debt: good debt and bad debt. Many of us know all too well what bad debt entails: putting yourself in financial jeopardy by purchasing items that you don't need and cannot afford. As we have seen, credit card debt is especially egregious because of the high interest rates attached to most cards.

Carrying good debt, on the other hand, is considered a desirable financial situation. Good debt can be defined as "anything you need but can't afford to pay for up front without wiping out cash reserves or liquidating all your investments" (CNNMoney, n.d. [b]). Good debt has everything to do with making wise financial decisions about

3

your future and should tie into your personal values and your long-term goals. Here are three examples of good debt.

▶ **BUYING A HOME.** This is likely the largest purchase you will ever make. Buying a home is an investment that will usually appreciate in value over time.

▶ **PAYING FOR COLLEGE.** There are many ways to pay for college, including college savings plans, college tax credits, and so on. The typical way to pay for college is with a student loan(s). Like a home, a college education is considered an investment that will get you further along in life because your education will give you greater job opportunities and earnings power.

▶ **PAYING FOR A CAR.** If you can pay for a car outright, go for it! This usually happens only with used cars, and a used car can bring all sorts of other issues with it. If you are planning on buying a new car, put down as much of a down payment as you possibly can (usually 10 percent is the minimum amount) without jeopardizing your other financial goals or tapping into your emergency fund (CNNMoney, n.d. [a]). This will be easier if you have been steadfastly putting money away each month to cover not only the down payment but also the operating and maintenance costs of the car going forward.

Later in this book, we will discuss the best ways to secure loans for the purchase of a college education.

THE BENEFITS AND DANGERS OF OWNING A CREDIT CARD

Credit cards offer tremendous benefits for consumers, including the ability to afford purchases big and small, in good times and bad (Federal Deposit Insurance Corporation, 2008). But owning one or more credit cards can also quickly bring financial peril with little or no effort and without malicious intent on the part of the credit card holder. Consider this scenario.

Suppose when you're 22 you charge $1,000 worth of clothes and CDs on a credit card with a 19 percent interest rate (also known as the **Annual Percentage Rate**, or APR). If you pay $20 against the balance each month, you'll be over 30 years old by the time you pay off the debt. You'll also have paid an extra $1,000 in interest during that time. And that's if you *never* charge anything else on that card.

Let's face it. Credit cards can be dangerous, really dangerous, but they don't need to be. The proper management of your credit cards will help you establish a solid credit score. And a good credit score, among other things, will afford you the opportunity to live your life in accordance with your personal values and long-term financial goals.

Here are some tips from the Federal Deposit Insurance Corporation when it comes to choosing and using credit cards:

▶ **CHOOSE THEM CAREFULLY.** Don't choose a card just because of the freebies that come with it or because there's no annual fee. Look for a card that's best for your borrowing habits. Ask yourself if you expect to pay your balance in full or if you'll routinely carry a balance on your card from month to month, which means you'll be charged interest. Generally speaking, if you expect to pay your credit card bill in full each month, your best bet is a card with no annual fee and with rebates or rewards that fit your lifestyle. If you don't expect to pay off your card balance in full most months, look for a card with a low interest rate and the right mix of rebates or rewards to justify any fees, including an annual fee.

Also, before you apply for a card, carefully review all other terms and conditions, which must be disclosed to you before you incur any charges on the account. Once you use a card, you have entered into a contract with the card issuer and you are obligated to abide by the terms disclosed to you.

▶ **USE THEM CAREFULLY.** Credit cards offer great benefits, especially the ability to buy now and pay later. But you must keep the debt levels manageable and pay on time. If you don't, the costs in terms of fees and interest, or the damage to your credit score, could be significant. Among the most important things to do are the following:

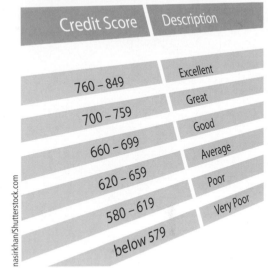

Credit Score Ratings

Credit Score	Description
760 – 849	Excellent
700 – 759	Great
660 – 699	Good
620 – 659	Average
580 – 619	Poor
below 579	Very Poor

nasirkhan/Shutterstock.com

Proper management of your credit cards will help ensure that you maintain great credit scores.

3

3

- **Understand your card's terms.** This is especially important when interest will be charged, so give particular attention to the interest rate. Be aware of circumstances that allow your card issuer to increase your interest rate.

- **Pay as much as you can to avoid or minimize interest charges.** If possible, pay your bill in full each month. Remember, paying only the minimum due each month means you'll be paying a lot of interest for many years with little reduction in the amount you owe. Those interest costs could far exceed the amount of your original purchase.

- **Pay on time to avoid late fees.** One option is to arrange for an automatic withdrawal from your checking account to cover your credit card bill and perhaps other recurring expenses (but be sure to record the transaction). Another option is to pay online, generally at least two days before the due date to be sure the payment is processed on time. If you pay by regular mail, allow enough time for delivery and processing by sending your payment about a week before the deadline.

- **Stay below your credit limit** to avoid penalties and a reduction in your credit score.

- **Read all the mailings from your card issuer.** They may include notices of an interest rate increase, a reduction in your credit limit, or other changes in your account.

- **Check for errors on your credit card bill.** If you find charges you didn't make, call your lender immediately to guard against fraud. Also, protect your rights under the law by mailing a letter to the card issuer's address for billing disputes (found on your credit card bill) within 60 days of the date of the bill. A phone call, fax, or e-mail isn't enough to fully protect you.

▶ **GUARD YOUR CREDIT CARD NUMBERS FROM THIEVES.** Never provide your credit card numbers—the account number and expiration date on the front and the security code on the back—in response to an unsolicited phone call, e-mail, or other communication you didn't originate. Also, never give out *any* personal information during any type of communication that you did not initiate. In general, only give your credit card or card numbers to reputable merchants or other organizations and preferably only when you initiate the transaction.

> ## success steps for taking charge of your credit cards
>
> • Choose them carefully.
> • Use them carefully.
>   • Understand your card's terms.
>   • Pay as much as you can to avoid or minimize interest charges.
>   • Pay on time to avoid late fees.
>   • Stay below your credit limit.
>   • Read all mailings from your card issuer.
>   • Check for errors on your credit card bill.
> • Guard your credit card numbers from thieves.

When using your credit card online, make sure you're dealing with a legitimate web site and that your information will be encrypted (scrambled for security purposes) during transmission (Federal Deposit Insurance Corporation, 2008). (Credit card fraud and identity theft are covered in more detail in a later section of this chapter.)

In addition to the advice given about choosing and using credit cards, it is equally important that you are aware of some recent changes to credit card laws (enacted in 2010) that can affect interest rates and fee increases on cards you already possess. The new laws are intended to protect consumers from sudden interest rate increases and other unfavorable changes in fees and account terms, but you should know about some potential pitfalls:

▶ **UNDERSTAND YOUR RIGHT TO CANCEL A CREDIT CARD BEFORE CERTAIN SIGNIFICANT ACCOUNT CHANGES TAKE EFFECT.** Under the new law, card issuers now must generally tell customers about certain changes in account terms—in areas such as interest rate and fee increases—45 days in advance, up from 15 days in the past. In that same notice, they must inform consumers of their right to cancel the card before certain account changes take effect. These notices may come with your credit card bill or through a separate communication.

Consumers who notify their card company to cancel their card before fees are increased or certain other significant changes

3

take effect are still required to pay their outstanding balance, but they cannot be required to pay it immediately. However, the card company can increase the minimum monthly payment, subject to certain limitations.

▶ **KEEP AN EYE ON YOUR CREDIT LIMIT.** Some people, even those with good credit histories, have recently seen their credit limits cut back. Reductions in credit lines can be harmful because your borrowing power becomes diminished. Also remember that your credit score is based, in part, on what percentage of your credit limit you are using and how much you owe. Borrowers who carry large balances in proportion to their credit limit may see their credit scores fall. A lower credit score can make it difficult or more expensive to get new credit in the future.

▶ **DECIDE HOW YOU WANT TO HANDLE TRANSACTIONS THAT WOULD PUT YOU OVER YOUR CREDIT LIMIT.** Under the new laws, no fees may be imposed for making a purchase or other transaction that would put your account over the credit limit unless you explicitly agree, in advance, that the credit card company can process these transactions for you and charge a fee.

▶ **BE CAUTIOUS WITH NO-INTEREST OFFERS.** Many retailers, such as electronics or furniture stores, promote credit cards with zero-percent interest for a certain amount of time. These cards allow you to buy big-ticket items, perhaps a sofa or a stereo system, without paying interest for anywhere from six months to more than a year. While the chance to avoid interest payments sounds like a terrific deal, keep in mind that if you don't follow the rules for these offers, this no-interest special could end up being expensive.

With many of these offers, you must pay off the *entire purchase* by the time the promotional period ends to take advantage of the zero-rate offer. If you don't, the lender charges you interest from the date you bought the item. You then have to pay interest—at the lender's standard rate—from the date of purchase. If the annual percentage rate, or APR, on the retailer's card is higher than what you would pay on another card you have, the extra costs could really add up. (Read more about APR in the next section.)

▶ **KEEP ONLY THE CREDIT CARDS YOU REALLY NEED, AND THEN PERIODICALLY USE THEM ALL.** Some consumers have too many credit cards, which generates the following concerns: Those extra cards can lead some people to overspend. Also, having many cards with no existing balance or a very low balance can reduce your credit score because prospective lenders can conclude that you have the *potential* to use them and get into debt.

For the average person, two or three general-purpose cards are probably enough. Consider cancelling and cutting up the rest. However, also remember that closing a credit card account can temporarily lower your credit score, especially if the cancelled card was one you owned and used responsibly for many years.

▶ **DO YOUR RESEARCH BEFORE PAYING HIGH ANNUAL FEES FOR A REWARDS CARD.** Rewards sound great in advertisements for credit cards, but the points system can be complicated, the rules are subject to change, and the benefits may not be as generous as you think. You should always read the fine print and be realistic about your likely use of the card before you accept an expensive annual fee in return for rewards.

▶ **TAKE ADDITIONAL PRECAUTIONS AGAINST INTEREST RATE INCREASES.** While card companies cannot increase the interest rate on *existing* balances except in certain circumstances, they can raise rates on extensions of credit for *new* purchases as long as proper notice is provided (Federal Deposit Insurance Corporation, 2010).

success steps for avoiding interest rate increases and fees on credit cards

- Understand your right to cancel a credit card before certain significant account changes take effect.
- Keep an eye on your credit limit.
- Decide how you want to handle transactions that would put you over your credit limit.
- Be cautious with no-interest offers.
- Keep only the credit cards you really need, and then periodically use them all.
- Do your research before paying high annual fees for a rewards card.
- Take additional precautions against interest rate increases.

3

UNDERSTANDING CREDIT CARD TERMINOLOGY

Financial terms (and there are *plenty* of them) can be confusing for the average consumer. Here are some terms with which you should become familiar because they pertain to credit cards. Use these terms when evaluating which card is right for you:

- ▶ **ANNUAL PERCENTAGE RATE (APR).** The APR is a measure of the cost of credit, expressed as a yearly interest rate. Usually, the lower the APR, the better for you. Be sure to check the fine print to see if your offer has a time limit. Your APR could be much higher after the initial limited offer.

- ▶ **GRACE PERIOD.** This is the time between the date of the credit card purchase and the date the company starts charging you interest.

- ▶ **ANNUAL FEES.** Many credit card issuers charge an annual fee for giving you credit, typically $15 to $59.

- ▶ **TRANSACTION FEES AND OTHER CHARGES.** Most creditors charge a fee if you don't make a payment on time. Other common credit card fees include those for cash advances and going beyond the credit limit. Some credit cards charge a flat fee every month, whether you use your card or not.

- ▶ **CUSTOMER SERVICE.** Customer service is something most people don't consider, or appreciate, until there's a problem. Look for a 24-hour, toll-free telephone number.

- ▶ **OTHER OPTIONS.** Creditors may offer other options for a price, including discounts, rebates, and special merchandise offers. If your card is lost or stolen, federal law protects you from owing more than $50 per card—but only if you report that it was lost or stolen within two days of discovering the loss or theft. Paying for additional protection may not be a good value (Federal Trade Commission, 2009).

THE MEANING OF CREDIT REPORTS

If you have a credit card, by definition, you have a credit report and a credit score (sometimes referred to as a credit rating or a FICO score). A credit report is a compilation of your payment history on all credit accounts and is a reflection of your financial activities. There are two types of credit reports:

▶ **AN INVESTIGATIVE REPORT.** This report is very detailed and may contain information about your lifestyle. Investigative reports are usually prepared for companies that want a thorough background check, such as one needed for high-dollar insurance policies, a high-level job, or a security clearance.

▶ **A STANDARD REPORT.** This report contains a complete outline of your financial history. You'll probably only have to deal with a standard report. A standard report has four parts:

- **Personal information.** Your name, spouse's name, address, previous addresses for the past five to ten years, date of birth, Social Security number (as well as that of your spouse), addresses of your previous and present employers, and your telephone number.

- **Payment history.** A list of your credit accounts, the opening date, whether you make timely payments, the balance, joint account information, and any negative information regarding the account.

- **Public record.** Monetary judgments, state and federal tax liens, and bankruptcies.

- **Inquiries.** Everyone who has viewed your credit report recently. One kind of inquiry is generated when you apply for credit, insurance, or a job. Another kind is a promotional inquiry that is created when lenders ask the credit bureau for lists of people who fit a certain category so they can mail them preapproved credit offers. A third kind of inquiry is created when lenders want to review their customers' credit reports to increase credit lines before the holidays. Customers who fit the stores' qualifications will be granted more credit (usa.gov, n.d.).

Credit Bureaus

Most credit reports are generated by three national credit-reporting agencies, or credit bureaus:

▶ Equifax
▶ Experian
▶ TransUnion

3

These agencies collect and sell information about your financial condition to companies if you are applying for a loan, applying for a job, or even renting an apartment. As a consumer, you are entitled to a free copy of your credit report (you must request it) from each of the three bureaus once every twelve months, as well as under certain other circumstances, such as if you've been denied credit or employment based on your credit report or if you believe you may be a fraud victim.

To order your free annual report from any of those three companies, there is only one place to go: visit www.AnnualCreditReport.com or call toll-free 1-877-322-8228. Remember to review each report carefully because the information in your file at each bureau may vary (the three bureaus do not share information). If you receive a notice that a lender or another entity used a credit report from a company other than one of these three credit bureaus, request your free copy from that bureau, too.

Once you obtain your report, review it for any inaccurate information and, if you find any, follow the procedures outlined by the credit bureau for disputing the information. The Federal Deposit Insurance Corporation recommends that you should review your credit report regularly (generally once a year), but it is particularly important to make sure your credit report is accurate before you apply for a loan because the information in your credit report determines your credit score (Federal Deposit Insurance Corporation, 2011).

CREDIT SCORES AND CREDITWORTHINESS

A credit score is an analysis of your creditworthiness based on your **credit history** and current credit accounts. Creditors use the credit-scoring system to help determine whether to give you credit and how much to charge you for it. Credit scores range from about 350 to 850 points. The higher the score, the more likely you are to get credit. A score of 700 and above is considered excellent, while borrowers with scores below 620 may not get the best interest rates available and may experience complications when requesting credit (usa.gov, n.d.).

Information about you and your credit experiences, like your bill-paying history, the number and type of accounts you have, late payments, collection actions, outstanding debt, and the age of your accounts, is collected from your credit application and your credit report. Using a statistical formula, creditors compare this information to the credit performance of consumers with similar profiles. A credit-scoring system awards points for each factor. A total number of points—a credit score—helps predict how creditworthy you are; that is, how likely it is that you will repay a loan and make the payments on time. Generally, consumers who are good credit risks have higher credit scores (Federal Trade Commission, 2011).

Why a Good Credit Score Matters

A good credit score is perhaps most important when you are planning to apply for a loan or to keep a good deal on a credit card. However, in these uncertain economic times, lenders are choosier about the loans they make and to whom they lend, so it's even more important to make sure your credit score is as high as possible.

The Federal Deposit Insurance Corporation offers the following tips for improving your credit reports and scores:

▶ **PAY YOUR LOANS AND OTHER BILLS ON TIME.** Even if you fell into trouble in the past, you can rebuild your credit history by beginning to make payments as agreed. Paying your debts on time has a positive effect on your credit score and can improve your access to credit. Don't ever pay a company that promises to clean up your credit record for a fee—they can't.

▶ **TRY TO MINIMIZE HOW MUCH YOU OWE IN RELATION TO YOUR CREDIT LIMIT.** This will help show that you are not overextended on debt.

▶ **IF YOU BELIEVE YOU CANNOT REPAY YOUR CREDITORS, CONTACT THEM IMMEDIATELY AND EXPLAIN YOUR SITUATION.** Ask about renegotiating the terms of your loan, including the amount you repay. Reputable credit-counseling organizations also can help you develop a personalized plan to solve your money problems, but less-reputable providers offer questionable or expensive services or make unsubstantiated claims (Federal Deposit Insurance Corporation, 2011).

3

> **success steps for improving your credit reports and scores**
>
> • Pay your loans and other bills on time.
> • Try to minimize how much you owe in relation to your credit limit.
> • If you believe you cannot repay your creditors, contact them immediately and explain your situation.

LAWS GOVERNING CREDIT CARD USE

Many federal laws are in place to protect your rights when you interact with your credit card company. Important laws and protections you should know about include the following:

▶ **THE CREDIT CARD ACT** (2009) provides many consumer credit protections. For example, your credit card company generally cannot increase the rate on your existing balance and must tell you 45 days before increasing the rate for new transactions. The Act also places new limits on fees and rate increases and requires consistency in payment dates and times.

▶ **THE EQUAL CREDIT OPPORTUNITY ACT** (1974) prohibits discrimination in credit transactions on the basis of certain personal characteristics, such as race, color, religion, national origin, sex, marital status, age, because you receive public assistance, or because you've exercised your rights under the Consumer Credit Protection Act.

▶ **THE FAIR CREDIT BILLING ACT** (1974) requires that a credit card company promptly credit your payments and correct mistakes on your bill without damage to your credit score. It also lets you dispute billing errors on your credit card and withhold payment for damaged goods.

▶ **THE FAIR CREDIT AND CHARGE CARD DISCLOSURE ACT** (1988) requires a lender offering you a credit card to tell you about certain terms on the card, such as the APR, the amount of any annual fee, and whether you have an interest-free period to pay your bill before any interest charges are added.

▶ **THE FAIR CREDIT REPORTING ACT** (1970) protects you against inaccurate or misleading information in credit files maintained by credit-reporting agencies. It requires that you must be told what's in your credit file and have the ability to correct any errors.

▶ **THE FAIR DEBT COLLECTION PRACTICES ACT** (1977) details the rules a debt collector must follow when trying to collect a debt from you. It prohibits collectors from engaging in abusive debt-collection practices, such as calling you outside the hours of 8:00 a.m. to 9:00 p.m. local time or communicating with you at work after they have been advised that this is unacceptable or prohibited by the employer.

▶ **THE TRUTH IN LENDING ACT** (1968) requires that lenders use uniform methods for computing the cost of credit and for disclosing credit terms so you can tell how much it will cost to borrow money. It also limits your liability to $50 if your credit card is lost, stolen, or used without your authorization, and it prohibits the unsolicited issuance of credit cards. The Fair Credit Billing Act and the Fair Credit and Charge Card Disclosures Act were later additions to the Truth in Lending Act, as are many provisions of the Credit CARD Act (Board of Governors of the Federal Reserve Board, 2010).

GETTING HELP IF YOU ARE IN OVER YOUR HEAD

No one plans to get into financial trouble when it comes to managing his or her credit cards. However, it does happen. If this describes your (unfortunate) situation, the Federal Trade Commission offers the following advice:

▶ **CONTACT YOUR CREDITORS.** If you're having trouble paying your bills, contact your creditors immediately. Tell them why it's difficult for you, and try to work out a modified plan that reduces your payments to a more manageable level. Don't wait until your accounts have been turned over to a debt collector. Take action immediately and keep a detailed record of your conversations and correspondence.

▶ **GET CREDIT COUNSELING.** Many universities, military bases, credit unions, and housing authorities operate nonprofit financial counseling programs. Some charge a fee for their services.

Creditors may be willing to accept reduced payments if you're working with a reputable program to create a debt-repayment plan. Before you choose a credit counselor, be sure to ask about fees you will have to pay and what kind of counseling you'll receive. A credit counseling organization isn't necessarily legitimate just because it says it's nonprofit. You may want to check with the Better Business Bureau for any complaints against a counselor or counseling organization. Visit www.bbbonline.org for your local Better Business Bureau's telephone number.

▶ **DECLARE BANKRUPTCY.** Bankruptcy is considered the credit solution of last resort. Unlike negative credit information that stays on a credit report for seven years, bankruptcies stay on a credit report for ten years. Bankruptcy can make it difficult to rent an apartment, buy a house or a condo, get some types of insurance, get additional credit, and, sometimes, get a job. In some cases, bankruptcy may not be an easily available option (Federal Trade Commission, 2009).

A word of caution when it comes to seeking outside help with your financial situation: Turning to a business that offers help in solving debt problems may seem like a reasonable solution when your bills become unmanageable. Be cautious. Before you do business with any company, check it out with your local consumer-protection agency or the Better Business Bureau in the company's location. One rule to remember is that if a credit-repair offer seems too easy or just too good to be true, it probably is. Knowing your rights can help you steer clear of rip-offs. For example, according to state and federal laws, companies that help people improve their credit rating cannot do the following:

▶ Make false claims about their services.

▶ Charge you until the services are completed.

▶ Perform services until the waiting period has passed. After you sign the written contract, you have three days to change your mind and cancel the services (Federal Trade Commission, 2009).

Be smart about who you contact, and more important, who may contact you first.

CREDIT CARD FRAUD AND IDENTITY THEFT

Identity theft involves someone else using your personal information to create fraudulent accounts, charge items to another person's existing accounts, or even get a job (Federal Trade Commission, 2011). Consider the following scenarios:

▶ A thief goes through trash to find discarded receipts or carbons and then uses your account numbers illegally.

▶ A dishonest clerk makes an extra imprint from your credit or charge card and uses it to make personal charges.

▶ You respond to a mailing or an e-mail asking you to call a long-distance number for a free trip or bargain-priced travel package. You're told you must join a travel club first and you're asked for your account number so you can be billed. The catch? Charges you didn't make are added to your bill, and you never get your trip.

Credit and charge card fraud costs cardholders and issuers hundreds of millions of dollars each year. While theft is the most obvious form of fraud, it can occur in other ways. For example, someone may

Blazej Lyjak/Shutterstock.com

Protect your identity and your financial situation by never giving out personal information unless it is to a trusted source.

use your card number without your knowledge (Federal Trade Commission, 1997). How can you prevent this from happening to you?

HOW TO PREVENT IT

It's not always possible to prevent credit or charge card fraud from happening. You can minimize the risks by managing your personal information wisely and cautiously. Protect yourself from identity theft by doing the following:

▶ **BEFORE YOU REVEAL ANY PERSONALLY IDENTIFYING INFORMATION, FIND OUT HOW IT WILL BE USED AND WHETHER IT WILL BE SHARED.**

▶ **PAY ATTENTION TO YOUR BILLING CYCLES.** Follow up with creditors if your bills don't arrive on time.

▶ **GUARD YOUR MAIL FROM THEFT.** Deposit outgoing mail in post office collection boxes or at your local post office. Promptly remove mail from your mailbox after it has been delivered. If you're planning to be away from home and can't pick up your mail, call or visit your local post office to request a vacation hold.

▶ **WHEN POSSIBLE, PUT PASSWORDS ON YOUR CREDIT CARD, BANK, AND PHONE ACCOUNTS.** Avoid using easily available information like your mother's maiden name, your birth date, the last four digits of your Social Security number or telephone number, or a series of consecutive numbers. It's a good idea to keep a list of your credit card issuers and their telephone numbers.

▶ **DON'T GIVE OUT PERSONAL INFORMATION ON THE TELEPHONE, THROUGH THE MAIL, OR OVER THE INTERNET UNLESS YOU'VE INITIATED THE CONTACT OR YOU KNOW WITH WHOM YOU'RE DEALING.**

▶ **PROTECT PERSONAL INFORMATION IN YOUR HOME.** Tear or shred documents like charge receipts, copies of credit offers and applications, insurance forms, physician's statements, discarded bank checks and statements, and expired credit cards before you throw them away. Be cautious about leaving personal information in plain view, especially if you have roommates, employ outside help, or are having service work done.

▶ **FIND OUT WHO HAS ACCESS TO YOUR PERSONAL INFORMATION AT WORK AND VERIFY THAT THE RECORDS ARE KEPT IN A SECURE LOCATION.**

▶ **NEVER CARRY YOUR SOCIAL SECURITY CARD; LEAVE IT IN A SECURE PLACE AT HOME.** Give out your Social Security number only when absolutely necessary.

▶ **ORDER YOUR CREDIT REPORT FROM EACH OF THE THREE MAJOR CREDIT-REPORTING AGENCIES EVERY YEAR TO MAKE SURE IT IS ACCURATE AND INCLUDES ONLY THOSE ACTIVITIES YOU'VE AUTHORIZED.**

▶ **CARRY ONLY THE IDENTIFICATION THAT YOU NEED** (Federal Trade Commission, 2011).

WHAT TO DO IF IT HAPPENS TO YOU

If you end up in the unfortunate situation where you lose your credit or charge cards or if you realize they've been lost or stolen, immediately call the issuer(s). Many companies have toll-free numbers and 24-hour service to deal with such emergencies (get the numbers from your monthly statement or the company's Web site). By law, once you

success steps for preventing credit card fraud and identity theft

- Don't reveal any personally identifying information until you find out how it will be used and whether it will be shared.

- Pay attention to your billing cycles.

- Guard your mail from theft.

- Put passwords on your credit card, bank, and phone accounts.

- Don't give out personal information on the telephone, through the mail, or over the Internet unless you've initiated the contact or you know with whom you're dealing.

- Protect personal information in your home.

- Find out who has access to your personal information at work.

- Never carry your Social Security card; leave it in a secure place at home.

- Order your credit report from each of the three major credit-reporting agencies every year to make sure it is accurate and includes only those activities you've authorized.

- Carry only the identification that you need.

report the loss or theft, you have no further responsibility for unauthorized charges. In any event, your maximum liability under federal law is $50 per card. Note, however, that you must report the loss or theft within two days of the discovery (Federal Trade Commission, 1997).

CASE IN POINT REVISITED

In the Case in Point presented at the beginning of this chapter, Hailey Mann assumed she would be able to get a loan to purchase a new car, only to find out that her credit score was too low and her credit report contained negative entries. When she requested and received a free credit report, she quickly realized that her credit card habits were negatively impacting her purchasing power and her ability to carry "good debt." Despite the uphill financial battle, Hailey made several important changes to her credit habits to reverse the damage done and to bring her in line with responsible handling of her credit.

CHAPTER SUMMARY

Chapter 3 provided you with information about the financial advantages and disadvantages of owning one or more credit cards and the impact the mismanagement of those cards can have on your financial well-being. You also learned about credit reports, credit scores, and credit bureaus and the bearing they have on your ability to secure a loan. Laws governing credit card use and credit card fraud and identity theft were also reviewed.

POINTS TO KEEP IN MIND

▶ It is important to identify the differences between positive financial behaviors and risky credit behaviors.
▶ All debt is not considered bad. Good debt—the kind that allows you to purchase a home or a car or finance a college education—is considered sound financial thinking.

▶ Good or bad credit reports and credit scores have a direct impact on your ability to make major purchases, secure loans, and even get a job.

▶ Several federal laws govern credit card use. They are all aimed at protecting the consumer.

▶ Budgeting, credit counseling, and bankruptcy are three options to consider if your mounting debt is no longer manageable.

▶ Credit card fraud and identity theft are two byproducts of credit card use. This chapter discussed several ways to prevent both from happening to you.

CRITICAL THINKING QUESTIONS

1. What are some additional risky credit behaviors people might exhibit that are not listed in this book?

2. What are some other examples of good debt?

3. If you own one or more credit cards, do you know the terms and conditions that come with each of them?

4. When was the last time you requested a free credit report (if you ever have)?

5. How careful are you about using your PIN at an ATM or in a store? Do you routinely check around you for onlookers before you key the number?

apply it!

 Activity #1: Personal Consumer Credit Report

GOAL: Learn how to read a sample credit report and interpret the data.

STEP 1: Review the following sample credit report.

STEP 2: Answer the questions about the report.

STEP 3: Discuss the answers as a class.

3

PERSONAL CONSUMER CREDIT REPORT	
This section contains the person's name and address, Social Security number, and date of birth. It also tells the previous address and employment information.	**Personal Identification Information** Name Social Security #: 123-45-6789 1234 Any Street Date of Birth: 02/26/1986 Dallas, TX 75000 Previous Address Employer: Acme, Inc. 456 Other Road Location: Dallas, TX Houston, TX 77000
This section contains publicly available information about legal matters related to credit. It might include judgments, tax liens, or bankruptcy history.	**Public Record Information** Dallas County Clerk Dallas, TX 75000 Civil Claim Status: Paid Amount: $1,000 Date: 04/05/2006
This section lists information about each credit account opened in the person's name. It identifies the lender and contains balance and payment information for the loan.	**Credit Account Information** ABC Auto Finance Account Number: 227744551 1000 Exchange Street Date Opened: 9/2007 San Antonio, TX 78000 Loan Type: Installment–Auto

Balance	$7,600
Credit Limit/Original Amount	$15,000
High Balance	N/A
Terms	60 months
Monthly Payment	$297
Past Due	0

My Bank   Account Number: 229933447
5000 Main Street   Date Opened: 8/2004
El Paso, TX 79000   Loan Type: Revolving credit card

Balance	$845
Credit Limit/Original Amount	$3,000
High Balance	$1,100
Terms	N/A
Monthly Payment	$20
Past Due	0

Gas Card of America   Account Number: 669900123
9999 Petroleum Street Date Opened: 12/2004
Fort Worth, TX 76000   Loan Type: Revolving credit card

Balance	$175
Credit Limit/Original Amount	$500
High Balance	$352
Terms	N/A
Monthly Payment	$20
Past Due	0

Account History:
60 days as of 6/2010
30 days as of 5/2010

This section lists information about anyone who has accessed this credit report.	**Recent Credit Inquiries** 01/2009 ABC Auto Finance 10/2010 Department Store, Inc. 08/2011 Home Loan Mortgage Company

1. What is the credit limit on the two revolving credit card accounts?

2. What is the person's current debt?

continued

3. Are any accounts past due?

4. Why would the Personal Identification Information (PII) be important to a lender?

5. Why would the Public Record Information be important to a lender?

6. Why would information in Credit Account Information be important to a lender?

7. Why would the information in Recent Credit Inquiries be important to a lender (Federal Reserve Bank of Dallas, n.d.)?

 Activity #2: Identity Theft Self-Check

GOAL: Determine how well you currently implement preventive credit card fraud and identity theft measures in your daily life.

STEP 1: Review each response in the list and indicate whether you perform this action always, sometimes, or never.

STEP 2: Tally your score and see how well you are taking measures to avoid credit card fraud and identity theft.

STEP	ALWAYS (2 POINTS)	SOMETIMES (1 POINT)	NEVER (0 POINTS)
Find out how personally identifying information will be used.			
Carry only the identification, checks, credit cards, or debit cards I really need.			

Password-protect my credit card, bank, and phone accounts.			
Shred documents with personal and financial information before disposing of or recycling them.			
Do not give out personal information over the phone, mail, or Internet unless I've initiated the contact.			
Verify who has my personal information at work.			
Review my credit report annually and identify and correct errors.			
Use secure mailboxes for incoming and outgoing mail.			
Avoid providing or sharing personal information (e.g., SSN) whenever possible.			
Total each column			
Grand Total			

Scores:

0–6: You are not taking many actions to minimize credit card fraud and identity theft. Consider how you can implement these and other steps to reduce your risk.

7–13: You have developed some good practices to avoid credit card fraud and identity theft; however, there is room for improvement. Consider what actions you need to take or apply more regularly to protect your identity.

14–18: You are doing a great job at minimizing the chances of your identity being compromised. Continue with this pattern and brainstorm additional ways to protect yourself.

CHECK YOUR UNDERSTANDING

 Visit www.cengagebrain.com to see how well you have mastered the material in Chapter 3.

3

REFERENCES

Board of Governors of the Federal Reserve System (2010). *Credit protection laws.* Retrieved December 22, 2011, from www.federalreserve.gov/creditcard/regs.html

CNNMoney (n.d. [a]). *Examples of good personal debt.* Retrieved December 19, 2011, from http://money.cnn.com/magazines/moneymag/money101/lesson9/index3.htm

CNNMoney (n.d. [b]). *Good debt vs. bad debt.* Retrieved December 19, 2011, from http://money.cnn.com/magazines/moneymag/money101/lesson9/index2.htm

Federal Deposit Insurance Corporation (FDIC Consumer News, Summer 2007). *51 ways to save hundreds on loans and credit cards.* Retrieved December 10, 2011, from www.fdic.gov/consumers/consumer/news/cnsum07/summer07bw.pdf

Federal Deposit Insurance Corporation (FDIC Consumer News, Spring 2005). *Five things you should know about . . . credit cards.* Retrieved December 12, 2011, from www.fdic.gov/consumers/consumer/news/cnspr05/spring_05_bw.pdf

Federal Deposit Insurance Corporation (FDIC Consumer News, Spring 2010). *New realities, new directions for credit cardholders.* Retrieved December 21, 2011, from www.fdic.gov/consumers/consumer/news/cnspr10/spring10BW.pdf

Federal Deposit Insurance Corporation (FDIC Consumer News, Winter 2008/2009). *Take charge of your credit cards.* Retrieved December 20, 2011, from www.fdic.gov/consumers/consumer/news/cnwin0809/win0809_bw.pdf

Federal Deposit Insurance Corporation (FDIC Consumer News, Fall 2011). *Your credit reports and credit scores: simple steps to make them better.* Retrieved December 20, 2011, from www.fdic.gov/consumers/consumer/news/cnfall11/Fall11BW.pdf

Federal Reserve Bank of Dallas Economic Education (n.d.). Building Wealth in the Classroom. *Take control of debt: are you creditworthy? Check your credit report.* Retrieved December 27, 2011, from www.dallasfed.org/assets/documents/educate/pubs/wealth_classroom/00_preface.pdf

Federal Trade Commission (1997). *Avoiding credit and charge card fraud.* Retrieved December 19, 2011, from www.ftc.gov/bcp/edu/pubs/consumer/credit/cre07.pdf

Federal Trade Commission (2009). *Getting credit: what you need to know about your credit.* Retrieved December 19, 2011, from www.ftc.gov/bcp/edu/pubs/consumer/credit/cre32.shtm

Federal Trade Commission (2011). *Building a better credit report.* Retrieved December 22, 2011, from www.ftc.gov/bcp/edu/pubs/consumer/credit/cre03.shtm

usa.gov (n.d.). *Credit reporting 101.* Retrieved December 22, 2011, from publications.usa.gov/USAFileDnld.php?Pub=pdf0293.pdf
http://publications.usa.gov/USAPubs.php?PubID=293

3

michaeljung/Shutterstock.com

CHAPTER OUTLINE

Types of Banks: Which One Is Right for You?

Retail Banks

Credit Unions

Online Banks

Other Types of Banks

4 Personal Banking

LEARNING OBJECTIVES

THE BIG PICTURE

Banks and banking services can have important differences, and it is to your advantage to find the types that best satisfy your personal banking needs. Chapter 4 addresses the options you have in this regard.

By the end of this chapter, you will achieve the following objectives:

▶ Review retail banks and the types of banking accounts and services available.

▶ Explain how credit unions differ from banks.

▶ Describe how online-only banks work.

▶ Identify other types of banks.

4

CHAPTER 4 CASE IN POINT

Jack Donahue is a transfer student at a college in South Florida. Previously, he attended a local community college near his hometown of Toledo, Ohio, but decided to transfer so he could further pursue his studies in marine biology. While he was in high school, Jack's parents had him open both a checking account and a savings account, which he still has. However, being so far away from home, Jack wanted the convenience of a local checking account as well as to avoid the hassle of writing out-of-state checks. He also wanted the ability to easily deposit his paychecks from the part-time job he took at the local food co-op. A friend recommended a bank near campus where Jack could open a checking account. Jack knew he wanted the convenience of online banking but was unsure of what services the bank offered and what account would be best for him and cost the least to maintain.

Imagine yourself in Jack's situation. Thoughtfully and honestly answer the following questions:

▶ How much do you know about the different types of accounts and services that are available from banks?

▶ Do you know the difference between a retail bank and a credit union?

▶ Can you identify the advantages and disadvantages of online-only banks?

▶ Do you know ways to minimize safety issues when it comes to online banking?

TYPES OF BANKS: WHICH ONE IS RIGHT FOR YOU?

Technology has changed the way we do many things in our lives, including how we bank. The advent of automatic teller machines (ATMs), debit cards, electronic banking, and telephone banking, for example, has revolutionized how we handle our money today. Given so many options, it can be difficult to navigate the waters of the financial services industry and decide what choices are best for you.

Even though you are just starting out on your own in life, whether you're in school, or working, or both, you have more than likely started a relationship with your local bank in some capacity. The chances are excellent that your local bank is a financial institution known as a retail bank.

RETAIL BANKS

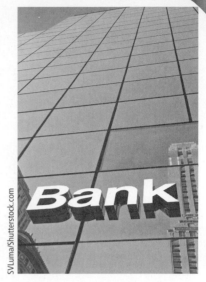

Retail banks are institutions that cater primarily to individuals. Your specific bank may be brick and mortar, with or without an online banking presence, or an online-only bank (see more about online-only banks later in this chapter). Regardless, retail banks offer a wide array of bank accounts and bank services to their customer base. Here are the most common ones you are likely using at your stage of life:

A retail bank is the type of bank you will most likely use.

TYPES OF ACCOUNTS

On your path to financial literacy, you have an advantage if you opened your own accounts or your parents steered you toward opening a checking and savings account before you started college or entered the work force. Even with limited funds and use, understanding the basic tenets of these accounts is paramount to you achieving financial stability and meeting your financial goals.

Checking Accounts

Your checking account is likely the single most important financial tool you have because you use it every day in some capacity. Be sure that the checking account you have gives you the best options for your needs and costs as little as possible to maintain.

Recent rule changes limit the fees banks and other financial institutions can charge on some services, which is welcome news for the consumer. However, with new laws and a challenging economy limiting banks' revenue, financial institutions are raising fees and reassessing features on services, including checking accounts (hence the bad news). That's why it is especially important to think about how you expect to use a checking account and then comparison shop for the right combination of convenience, costs, and services (FDIC, 2011).

Roman Sigaev/Shutterstock.com

Retail banks offer a wide variety of services, including automated teller machines (ATMs).

It's hard to predict how banks will change their fees and policies for checking and savings accounts, so the Federal Deposit Insurance Corporation (FDIC) recommends the following basic strategies to keep costs down:

▶ **COMPARISON SHOP SO YOU DON'T PAY MORE THAN NECESSARY FOR ACCOUNTS.** Look at what your bank and a few competitors are offering. If your bank is among those that eliminated free checking services, you may still be able to find another bank offering them, especially if you sign up for direct deposit and electronic statements or if you conduct a certain number of transactions each month. It should be noted that under Federal Reserve Board rules, an institution can't advertise a free checking account if you could be charged a maintenance fee or an activity fee—for example, a penalty for going below a required minimum balance. Your bank can, however, offer a free account and still impose charges for certain services, such as check printing, ATM use, or overdrafts.

Some banks may be adding or raising minimum balance requirements. One alternative is to ask yourself if you can get by with a no-frills checking account. This account typically offers basic banking services without a minimum balance requirement or a monthly maintenance fee but may limit the number of checks you write or your monthly ATM or debit card transactions.

When you see some accounts that are good possibilities, call, e-mail, or visit the institutions and ask questions to find the account that offers the best rates, features, and the lowest fees.

In today's low-interest-rate environment, it might be better to choose a free account that pays no interest or only a small amount of interest instead of selecting an account that pays a modest interest rate but imposes a monthly fee. Similarly, it may be better to maintain a balance and avoid a monthly fee rather than putting that money in an account paying a modest interest rate. In both cases, any interest you earn would probably be a lot less than the monthly fee, which can be $10 or higher.

Also, understand what you can lose if you do not meet the terms and conditions of the account. Before you open a new account, read all the information about it, including the fine print. You do not want to be surprised later by limitations and fees you could have avoided.

Similarly, ask your bank how it calculates the account balance for purposes of meeting a required minimum. "Some banks will charge a fee if the account balance falls below the minimum at any point during a month, while others charge a fee if the account's average daily balance during the month is below the minimum," states Heather St. Germain, a Consumer Affairs Specialist at the FDIC. "Understanding the rules will make them easier to follow and will help you avoid fees."

▶ **PROTECT AGAINST UNEXPECTED COSTS BY MONITORING COMMUNICATIONS FROM YOUR BANK.** Whether you keep track of your account online or on paper, it's a good idea to promptly check account statements for errors that can cost you money, fees you didn't realize you were running up, and account changes you forgot about or didn't notice in the mailings from your bank.

It's also important to review your account statement as soon as you receive it to identify and dispute unauthorized transactions.

4

Better yet, check your account activity online periodically instead of waiting for the statement to arrive in the mail. Consider signing up for electronic statements if your bank offers them. "That way, you'll get an e-mail notifying you about your latest statement online, which can be a good reminder to promptly review your account," said St. Germain.

Paying attention to account activity is also crucial if unauthorized transactions occur. In particular, if your debit or ATM card is lost or stolen, your liability for unauthorized charges is limited under federal law based on how quickly you report a problem. To get the most protection, you must notify your bank within two business days of learning that the card is missing.

In addition to reviewing account statements, read any other mail or e-mail from your bank. These communications may contain notices of important account changes, including increases in fees or penalties

▶ **IF OVERDRAWING YOUR ACCOUNT IS AN ONGOING PROBLEM, LOOK INTO ALTERNATIVES TO HIGH-COST OVERDRAFT PROGRAMS.** By far, the best and cheapest way to avoid overdrafts is to keep a good record of your transactions—all of your deposits and withdrawals, including direct deposits, automatic transfers, ATM transactions, and debit card purchases—and have enough funds in your account to cover your anticipated withdrawals.

As part of your system for keeping track of your account, find out if your bank will send you an e-mail or text message alerting you when a significant transaction posts to your account (such as a recurring automatic payment) or if your balance drops below a specific amount. This alert service, which is offered free at many banks, enables you to consider moving funds to your checking account from a savings account so you can avoid overdrawing your account. Be sure to understand the potential costs, if any.

In recent years, banks have offered overdraft programs that—for a high fee—automatically approved debit card and ATM transactions when the balance dipped below zero. Under new rules that went into effect in 2010, banks must ask customers if they want to pay for overdraft coverage for debit card purchases and

ATM withdrawals. If you agree to this coverage, your bank can charge you a fee to process these transactions when they exceed your account balance. If you don't opt in, expect that these debit card and ATM transactions will be declined; however, you will avoid paying an overdraft or insufficient funds fee.

Keep in mind that these new limitations apply *only* to one-time debit card transactions and ATM withdrawals. That means, for example, that your bank may cover an overdraft that occurs by check or automatic payment (such as for your mortgage, insurance premiums, or health-club membership) without you opting in for overdraft coverage, and it is likely to charge you a fee for doing so.

In addition, remember that if the bank returns a check or automatic payment instead of covering it, you may encounter additional difficulties beyond the bank's fee. For instance, the merchant that initially accepted the bounced check may charge a fee for the returned item and refuse to accept checks from you in the future.

If you often overdraw your checking account and you'd rather pay a fee than have a purchase declined, consider avoiding your bank's overdraft coverage and asking about less-expensive options instead. Among the possibilities are the following:

- Link your checking account to a savings account so that, for a small fee, money is automatically moved to cover overdrafts.

- Prearrange for an overdraft line of credit, which is an automatic loan triggered by a shortfall in your checking account. This loan will generally be less expensive than overdraft coverage, especially if you incur several overdrafts and pay a separate fee each time, but look into the costs for both options.

- If you're facing a short-term cash crunch, ask your bank and a couple of others if they offer an affordable small-dollar loan to cover your expenses.

If you struggle with overdrafts despite your best efforts to avoid them, and if you do not plan to participate in one of these

4

lower-cost options, research what your bank and others may charge for covering overdrafts.

▶ **MINIMIZE FEES AT THE ATM.** Most banks don't charge their customers to use the bank's ATMs. So do your best to get cash at your bank or one of your bank's machines.

When you need cash and you're not near your bank or one of its ATMs, know your options. You especially want to avoid paying two fees—one to your bank and one to another bank for using its ATM.

One option is to use your debit card when making a purchase and ask for cash back. This is also a good choice if your bank charges a fee for exceeding a certain number of ATM transactions in a month. However, first confirm with your bank that getting cash back on a debit card transaction is free. Be sure to record the purchase as well as the cash withdrawal so you don't overdraw your account (FDIC, 2010).

---

success steps for keeping checking account costs down

- Comparison shop so you don't pay more than necessary for accounts.
- Protect against unexpected costs by monitoring communications from your bank.
- If overdrawing your account is an ongoing problem, look into alternatives to high-cost overdraft programs.
- Minimize fees at the ATM.

Savings Accounts

As you have learned, it is never too early to start saving, nor is it ever too late to start saving. If you have been an early bird about paying yourself first and have started some sort of savings plan, good for you! If not, now is the time to make your savings plan a part of your overall financial strategy.

One of the easiest ways to save money but still have ready access to it is to open some type of savings account through your bank or other financial institution. Also known as a **deposit account**, a savings account can come in several different forms:

▶ **TRADITIONAL SAVINGS ACCOUNT.** A traditional savings account can be opened at your local bank or credit union (credit unions are covered later in this chapter), or you can arrange to open an online savings account through any national, regional, or local bank. Traditional savings accounts generally pay higher rates than an interest-bearing checking account. Online savings accounts that do not have a physical presence often have better interest rates than their brick-and-mortar counterparts because they do not have the same overhead costs. There is generally a three-day waiting period before you can access your funds through an online savings account, so take that into consideration. One of the best features of a traditional savings account is that your money is liquid (accessible to you at any time). In exchange for that liquidity, these types of accounts do not pay as high a **yield** (the annual rate of return on an investment) as other types of deposit accounts.

▶ **CERTIFICATES OF DEPOSIT.** A **certificate of deposit**, also known as a CD, is an interest-earning savings instrument purchased for a fixed period of time. Certificates of deposit remain some of the safest and most reliable places for your money. But as with most financial products and services, it pays to do some research and take other precautions before you buy.

CDs come in many varieties, so shop around. With a traditional FDIC-insured CD, you agree to keep the money in an account for a set term—a few weeks to several years. In return, the bank agrees to pay you a higher interest rate than you would receive from a checking or savings account. If you need the money earlier, you can arrange that, but expect to pay an early withdrawal penalty. However, the traditional CD is only one of the choices that are offered (FDIC, 2009).

The traditional CD has three common variations of which you should be aware:

• **Bump-up CDs** enable a depositor to choose to switch mid-term to a higher interest rate if market rates go up.

4

- **Step-up CDs** allow for periodic, predetermined increases in interest rates.

- **Liquid CDs** have fixed interest rates but permit the depositor to withdraw a portion of the original deposit early without paying a penalty.

How can you choose a CD wisely, especially if you're considering a nontraditional kind? First, think about how much money you're willing to keep untouched at the bank and for how long. Remember that if you have to withdraw the funds before maturity, you will pay a penalty, usually a loss of some or all of the interest you've earned—and perhaps even some of your principal (the amount you deposited originally).

Next, shop around for the highest interest rates for the CD amount and time period you're considering. In general, the larger the deposit and the longer the maturity, the more interest you can expect to earn.

When you shop, check with at least three or four CD providers, including institutions you already deal with and trust. Find out about interest rates, minimum deposit requirements, maturity dates, and early withdrawal provisions. Remember that these features can vary widely from bank to bank. The important thing is to try to understand the key terms and conditions of the CD and what they could mean for you (FDIC, 2005).

▶ **MONEY MARKET ACCOUNTS.** A **money market account** is an interest-earning account that pays relatively high interest rates and offers limited check-writing privileges. Money market accounts come in five different forms:

- **Super NOW account.** This is a government-insured money market account, is offered by depository institutions, and is a high-interest **NOW (negotiable order of withdrawal) account.** The initial minimum deposit ranges from $1,000 to $2,500. Depositors can withdraw their funds at any time without penalty.

- **Money market deposit accounts (MMDA).** This type of government-insured account is also offered through depository institutions. MMDAs carry minimum-balance requirements and tiered interest rates that vary with the size of the account balance. The customer usually has to deposit $1,000 to open an account. MMDAs usually pay higher interest rates than super NOW accounts.

- **Asset management accounts (AMA).** Also known as all-in-one accounts and central asset accounts, AMAs collect most of a customer's monetary asset accounts into one unified package and report them on a single monthly statement. AMAs are offered through depository institutions, stock brokerage firms, financial services companies, and mutual funds. Typically, $10,000 spread across all subaccounts is required to open an AMA (Garman & Forgue, 2010).

BANKING SERVICES

By now, you are aware that banks offer a wide variety of services that go beyond opening bank accounts. Some of these services may include different types of loans for the purchase of a vehicle or a home, safety deposit boxes, lines of credit, investment vehicles (stocks and bonds), and so on. At your age, it's likely that you already take advantage of one or both of the following new services that many (if not most) banks offer. However, as with any type of banking service, you must take precautions to protect yourself when using online and mobile banking services.

Online Banking

Online banking, bill paying, and shopping are conveniences that most people want to enjoy. Most of the time, high-tech transactions are completed quickly and without a glitch. However, just as with other transactions, in a small percentage of cases, something goes wrong. That's why you need to take precautions against theft and errors.

In particular, even as banks and merchants tighten up security, Internet thieves devise new, sophisticated ways to trick consumers into sending money or into revealing information that can be used to commit fraud. The Federal Deposit Insurance Corporation offers these strategies to protect your money while banking online:

▶ **IF YOU BANK ONLINE, FREQUENTLY CHECK YOUR DEPOSIT ACCOUNTS AND LINES OF CREDIT TO SPOT AND REPORT ERRORS OR FRAUDULENT TRANSACTIONS, JUST AS YOU SHOULD WITH TRADITIONAL BANKING.** Check your accounts online about

4

once or twice a week. Fortunately, more and more banks are making it easier for their customers to keep an eye on their accounts electronically. For example, many banks offer e-mail or text message alerts when your balance falls below a certain level or when there is a transaction over a certain amount.

Federal laws generally limit your liability for unauthorized electronic funds transfers, especially if you report the problem to your financial institution within specified time periods, which vary depending on the circumstances. A good rule of thumb is to check your statements promptly and report unauthorized transactions to your bank as soon as possible.

▶ **NEVER GIVE YOUR SOCIAL SECURITY NUMBER, CREDIT OR DEBIT CARD NUMBERS, PERSONAL IDENTIFICATION NUMBERS (PINS), OR ANY OTHER CONFIDENTIAL INFORMATION IN RESPONSE TO AN UNSOLICITED E-MAIL, TEXT MESSAGE, OR PHONE CALL, NO MATTER WHO THE SOURCE SUPPOSEDLY IS.** Chances are high that an urgent e-mail or phone call appearing to be from a government agency (such as the IRS or the FDIC), a bank, merchant, or other well-known organization may be a scam attempting to trick consumers into divulging personal and account information. It's called *phishing*, a high-tech variation of the concept of fishing for personal information.

Also watch out for phishing scams that involve bogus text messages sent to cell phones claiming that a bank account has been blocked and the recipient must call a certain number to fix the problem. If you make that call, you likely will be asked to enter your account number and PIN. Criminals can use this information to make counterfeit debit cards and drain your account.

▶ **DON'T OPEN ATTACHMENTS OR CLICK ON LINKS IN UNSOLICITED E-MAILS FROM ANYONE YOU DON'T KNOW OR YOU OTHERWISE AREN'T SURE ABOUT.** Sometimes these attachments or links can infect your computer with spyware that can change your security settings and record your keystrokes. Spyware can secretly steal your passwords, bank or credit card numbers, and your answers to security questions like your mother's maiden name or your high school. Online thieves can use this information to log into your account, make changes, and transfer money, leaving your bank account empty.

▶ **WATCH OUT FOR POP-UP WINDOWS ASKING FOR PERSONAL INFORMATION OR WARNING OF A VIRUS.** This is called scareware because it frightens people into providing information or downloading malicious software or paying for its removal. If you get an e-mail or pop-up window saying your computer has a virus and it offers a program to clean your PC—and the warning window won't go away—your first step is to use the computer's task manager function and click "end task" or "force quit" to shut the pop-up window. Scareware can be a nuisance to clean off your computer, so call your antivirus software company if you need help (and you do have antivirus software loaded on your machine, don't you?).

▶ **USE A MIX OF SECURITY TOOLS AND PROCEDURES.** At the top of the list of security tools to use—and keep updated—is antivirus software to detect and block spyware and other malicious attacks and a firewall to stop hackers from accessing your computer. Even if your computer seems fine, schedule an automatic antivirus scan to run at least once a week but preferably every day. Call or e-mail your antivirus vendor right away if you get a warning message and you don't know what to do next.

Also consider these extra precautions as you use the Internet:

- *Don't log into your bank account while using public computers, such as at a library, or free wireless connections at coffee shops and similar places.* Criminals often try passwords from these locations.

- *Pay attention to the toolbars at the top of your screen.* Current versions of the most popular Internet browsers and search engines often will indicate if you are visiting a suspicious Web site.

- *Choose strong user IDs and passwords that will be easy for you to remember but hard for hackers to guess.* The strongest ones have a combination of letters, numbers, and other characters, and are at least 10 characters long. For your online banking, choose IDs and passwords that are different from those you use for e-mails or social networking sites, just in case they get into the wrong hands. Also change

4

your online banking password about every 90 days. If you remove a computer virus from your PC, immediately change your password.

- *Have each person in your household bank and shop online and send e-mail through his or her own standard user account.* Not conducting these online activities through the computer's administrator account—the one that makes changes affecting all users—reduces the likelihood that a hacker can install unwanted programs on your PC. Limit the use of the administrator account to special tasks needed for your computer, such as adding or removing software and installing updates to your operating system.

- *Consider using a separate computer solely for online banking or shopping.* A growing number of people are purchasing basic PCs and using them only for banking online and not Web browsing, e-mailing, social networking, playing games, or other activities that increase the chances of downloading malicious software. You can also consider using an old PC for this limited purpose, but you should uninstall any software you no longer need and follow up with a scan of the entire PC to check for malicious software.

- *Use security products only from reputable companies.* One way to check out these products is by reading reviews from computer and consumer publications. Look for a product that has high ratings for detecting problems and for providing tech support if your computer becomes infected.

▶ **BEWARE OF CHECK SCAMS.** With unemployment high, con artists are preying on people who need cash. One common check scam involves attractive offers—usually originating in e-mails or online job postings—involving part-time work from home. As the new employee, you will be sent a check to deposit (which will be counterfeit) and told to forward cash from your own account (to the crooks). Another scam involves mystery shopper programs where the new hire is given fake money orders or checks and asked to wire funds to the criminals. Unlike electronic transfers that are covered by consumer protection laws, fraudulent check scams often leave consumers suffering the loss.

▶ **WHEN SHOPPING ONLINE, DEAL WITH REPUTABLE MERCHANTS AND BE WARY OF UNBELIEVABLY LOW PRICES.** There is no guaranteed way to ensure that an online merchant you're unfamiliar with is reputable, but you can avoid doing business with an unreliable one. First ask your friends and family if they've had good experiences with a merchant you're considering using. Second, you may already know and like some online merchants from their retail outlets, mail-order catalogs, or other services. They are likely to be a safer bet than an unfamiliar merchant that doesn't list a physical address or a phone number on its Web site.

If you are uncertain about an online merchant, check with the Better Business Bureau Online (www.bbbonline.com). You can also search online for complaints about the business. Similarly, if you have a problem with an online merchant, file a report with the Better Business Bureau. The Bureau will notify the merchant about your concern and ask you if the issue was resolved. A legitimate merchant will attempt to fix the problem, while a crooked company may have many unresolved issues.

▶ **USING A CREDIT CARD GENERALLY OFFERS MORE PURCHASE PROTECTION THAN A DEBIT CARD OR OTHER ELECTRONIC FORMS OF ONLINE PAYMENT.** Unlike paying with a debit card and the money being immediately transferred out of your account, with a credit card you generally have weeks to pay your bill. If the merchant does not deliver as promised, then you have time to dispute the transaction and even enlist the help of your credit card company. Federal law gives you certain rights in areas such as dispute resolution when buying with a credit card.

▶ **BE ON GUARD AGAINST SCAMS HIDING BEHIND ONLINE COUPON OFFERS.** Web sites for legitimate coupons will ask consumers to provide only an e-mail address to use their service to search for online specials and discounts. Beware of any coupon site that asks for personal, financial, or payment information, which can be misused by criminals (FDIC, 2009).

4

success steps for protecting your money while banking online

- Frequently check your deposit accounts and lines of credit to spot and report errors or fraudulent transactions.
- Never give out confidential information in response to an unsolicited e-mail, text message, or phone call.
- Don't open attachments or click on links in unsolicited e-mails from anyone you don't know or you otherwise aren't sure about.
- Watch out for pop-up windows asking for personal information or warning of a virus.
- Use a mix of security tools and procedures.
- Be aware of check scams.
- When shopping online, deal with reputable merchants and be wary of unbelievably low prices.
- Using a credit card generally offers more purchase protection than a debit card or other electronic forms of online payment.
- Be on guard against scams hiding behind online coupon offers.

Mobile Banking

Nine out of ten Americans have a cell phone and, according to research by The Nielsen Company, more than half of them will be using a smartphone by the end of 2011 (are you one of them?). A smartphone is actually a handheld computer that enables users to access the Internet, run applications, and make phone calls. For a steadily increasing number of consumers, smartphones can also be used for banking.

Banking over a cell phone isn't fantasy; it's a reality that many banks are offering their customers to check their balance, find the nearest ATM, and even pay bills. It means increased convenience and flexibility, especially for people who do a lot of traveling. For example, many banks can send alerts to customers' smartphones advising them if they are about to overdraw their account or if the bank has detected suspicious activity.

The Web-based version of mobile banking, in which customers access the bank's Web site using the browser on their smartphone, is the most prevalent option. However, application-based services, in which customers download specific software that runs on their phone, are quickly becoming popular because they are more user-friendly. What should you do if you are interested in mobile banking by smartphone?

▶ **ASK YOUR BANK IF IT OFFERS THE SERVICE AND IF THERE'S A COST.** As with online banking, most banks don't charge customers extra for mobile banking, but you should not assume that it's free.

▶ **TAKE SECURITY PRECAUTIONS.** Make sure that your phone or the mobile-banking application you'd be using is password protected. That way, if you lose your phone, someone else can't access your bank account without having your password.

Confirm with your bank that account numbers, passwords, and other sensitive details are not stored on the phone where a thief could retrieve them. Another thing to remember is that both Web- and application-based mobile banking systems are more secure than those that use text messaging. You may also want to consider purchasing antivirus software to run on your phone because it's only a matter of time before viruses that attempt to infect your home computer migrate to smartphones.

▶ **BEFORE YOU SIGN UP FOR ANY MOBILE BANKING SERVICE, MAKE SURE YOU UNDERSTAND WHAT'S AT RISK IF SOMETHING GOES WRONG.** Some banks and other companies offer the option to use your smartphone to transfer relatively small amounts of money to friends and family. These are called person-to-person, or P2P, payments, and you should not only ask what fees are associated with them but you should also understand what happens if a payment gets sent to the wrong person.

To learn more about mobile banking, start with your bank's Web site to see what services are offered and how they are provided. Ask your friends and family if they use mobile banking and what they think of it. And, as with any other product or

4

4

service, make sure you understand how it works so you can make an informed decision about whether mobile banking may be right for you (FDIC, 2010).

CREDIT UNIONS

Credit unions (CU) are member-owned, not-for-profit, federally insured financial institutions that provide checking, savings, and loan services to members. People all over the world belong to credit unions, including over 91 million members in the United States. Because credit unions are not-for-profit financial institutions, their focus is only on serving the financial needs of members. On the whole, credit unions typically offer higher rates on savings, fewer fees, and lower rates on loans. Here's what you can expect from a credit union:

▶ **ACCESSIBLE TO MOST AMERICANS.** To join a credit union, you must be eligible for membership. Members of each credit union share a common bond, such as having the same employer, belonging to an organization or church, or living in the same community. Some credit unions serve multiple groups with different common bonds. Each credit union determines the specific group or field of membership it will serve.

▶ **PERSONAL SERVICE.** Credit unions provide personal service designed to help members grow their savings, pay off debt, and plan for the future.

▶ **NOT-FOR-PROFIT FOCUS.** Credit unions are member owned and operated, not-for-profit organizations. This enables them to fairly price products and services as well as offer competitive interest rates.

▶ **COMMUNITY SPIRIT.** Because credit union members have a common geographic area, workplace, or other association, they often have shared interests and appreciate participating in an institution designed to help other members.

▶ **FEWER FEES.** Credit unions tend to offer fewer and sometimes reduced fees for their products and services, compared to those of other financial service institutions because of their not-for-profit, cooperative structure.

▌ **EXPANDED SERVICES.** Credit unions have been able to keep pace with the needs of their members by offering a variety of products and services in addition to savings and consumer loans:

- Direct deposit
- Financial education and counseling
- Electronic banking
- ATMs
- **Automated Clearing House (ACH)** origination
- Overdraft protection
- Home equity loans
- Mortgage loans
- Member business loans

Most credit unions either offer free access to a large network of ATMs or provide reimbursement for fees incurred when using other institutions' machines.

▌ **SHARED INCOME.** Credit unions return surplus income to their members in the form of dividends.

▌ **INSURED DEPOSITS.** Through the National Credit Union Share Insurance Fund (NCUSIF), the funds of all federal and most state-chartered credit union members are insured up to $250,000 per individual depositor, per the federally insured credit union (National Credit Union Administration, n.d.).

ONLINE BANKS

As you have learned, many traditional brick-and-mortar banks have established an online banking presence, allowing customers to choose when and how they will do their banking. In this hybrid approach, customers have the convenience of anytime banking, as well as the face-to-face customer service that many consumers still desire.

In today's world, another type of banking structure has emerged that continues to gain momentum, and that is the concept of online-only banks.

Like their brick-and-mortar counterparts, online banks offer anytime banking. In addition, and this is their biggest draw, online

4

OLJ Studio/Shutterstock.com

Online-only banking may be an attractive option for your banking needs.

banks usually offer higher interest rates on both checking and savings accounts because they do not have the same overhead costs as traditional banks.

If you decide that an online bank is the best option for you, it's wise to check out competitive rates before signing up for any services. Several Web sites are dedicated to monitoring bank rates on a daily basis (see Appendix A in this book for a list of related Web sites) and can aid in your decision making. You should also make sure that the online bank you choose offers the full gamut of the services you need because not all online banks are as full service as traditional banks.

You might be steered away from an online-only bank for some of the following reasons:

▶ **CUSTOMER SERVICE CAN BE POOR.** You never have face-to-face contact with a representative, so your ability to get your issues resolved may be hit or miss, and you won't likely talk to the same person twice.

▶ **CHECK CLEARING AND DEPOSITS MAKE TAKE LONGER.** It sounds contrary to the notion that online equals speed, but, in reality, it can take a couple of business days for your transactions to go through.

▶ **TECHNICAL DIFFICULTIES.** It's a fact that Web sites falter. If that happens, you can't go to your local branch, and the 800 number will be jammed (Pritchard, n.d.).

If you don't mind the potential risks to online-only banking, it may be a wise choice for you.

OTHER TYPES OF BANKS

While the chances are good that you have dealt only with your retail bank or credit union to date, you may have a need in your financial future to interface with one or more of the following banks. As with any banking relationship, be sure to shop around and compare which services and products best fit your needs.

▶ **COMMERCIAL BANKS.** Also known as business banks, commercial banks are entities that have a financial relationship only with businesses.

▶ **INVESTMENT BANKS.** Investment banks deal with **capital markets**, as in the stock market.

▶ **SAVINGS AND LOAN INSTITUTIONS.** Savings and loan institutions primarily provide financing for long-term residential mortgages.

CASE IN POINT REVISITED

In the Case in Point presented at the beginning of this chapter, Jack Donahue was in the market for a checking account at a local bank near his college in South Florida. He knew he wanted the convenience of online banking, but he knew little else about the types of accounts and services the bank offered. One of his main goals was to open an account that would cost him the least to maintain.

Jack sat down with an account manager at the bank to discuss his options. After a short conversation about Jack's banking needs, the account manager recommended that Jack open a no-fee or low-fee checking account with no minimum balance and overdraft protection. Jack also applied for a debit card, and once the account was opened, he registered for online banking privileges at no cost.

CHAPTER SUMMARY

In Chapter 4, you were introduced to the world of personal banking, retail banking specifically. Various types of bank accounts and banking services were emphasized, along with suggestions for keeping your money safe and secure. Online and mobile banking and online-only banks were highlighted as the new wave of banking, and the pros and cons of these services were identified. Finally, other types of banks were briefly discussed.

POINTS TO KEEP IN MIND

▶ Several types of financial institutions are available to consumers, but retail banks are the most common.

▶ Retail banks offer many options for the types of bank accounts and banking services they offer.

▶ Online and mobile banking are two emerging ways to do banking. Both choices come with caveats for safety and security.

▶ Credit unions are another alternative to traditional banks. You must be a member of a community that is served by the credit union in order to join.

▶ Credit unions often offer higher interest rates and lower fees to members.

▶ Online-only banks are an attractive option for some customers. While interest rates are often higher than traditional banks, not all online-only banks offer a full range of services.

▶ Other types of banks with which you may interface in your lifetime are commercial banks, investment banks, and savings and loan institutions.

CRITICAL THINKING QUESTIONS

1. What are some advantages of online-only banking? Disadvantages?

2. Why do you think it is important to do some research before opening any type of checking or savings account?

3. Would you consider joining a credit union if you became a member of that credit union's community? Why?

4. In what ways will you try to minimize the need for overdraft protection and hefty bank fees?

5. What are some possible caveats for using online and mobile banking? What can you do to protect yourself from potential problems?

4

apply it!

 Activity #1: Comparison Shopping

GOAL: Research and recognize the best rates on certificates of deposit.

STEP 1: Conduct an Internet search to find Web sites that offer information on competitive rates for certificates of deposit (alternatively, several Web sites that offer this service are listed in Appendix A of this book).

STEP 2: Using the following table, chart interest rates, minimum deposit requirements, maturity dates, and early withdrawal provisions on a one-year certificate of deposit for each of four banks. Be sure to include your current bank (even if you do not have a CD there) as one of your options.

STEP 3: Be prepared to share your findings with your class, and to discuss which bank CD option you would choose and why.

Financial Institution	Interest Rate	Minimum Deposit Requirements	Maturity Dates	Early Withdrawal Provisions

 Activity #2: Web Research

GOAL: Gain an understanding of how to use the Better Business Bureau's Web site.

STEP 1: Log on to the better Business Bureau's Web site at www.bbbonline.com and click on the "For Consumers" link.

STEP 2: Click on the "Business Reports" link on the next page.

STEP 3: Enter the pertinent information from the four banks that you queried about certificate of deposit information in the previous activity in the Search for and In boxes.

STEP 4: Write a report detailing what you found out about the four banks. Be sure to include whether the report on each bank might influence your decision to open a CD account at any of them.

CHECK YOUR UNDERSTANDING

Visit www.cengagebrain.com to see how well you have mastered the material in Chapter 4.

REFERENCES

Federal Deposit Insurance Corporation (FDIC Consumer News, Summer 2010). *Bank accounts are changing: what you need to know.* Retrieved January 5, 2012, from www.fdic.gov/consumers/consumer/news/cnsum10/Summer10BW.pdf

Federal Deposit Insurance Corporation (FDIC Consumer News, Summer 2005). *Bank CDs: new options, more flexibility for stashing your cash.* Retrieved January 4, 2012, from www.fdic.gov/consumers/consumer/news/cnsum05/bankcds.html

Federal Deposit Insurance Corporation (FDIC Consumer News, Winter 2010/2011). *Calling all smartphone users: are you ready for mobile banking?* Retrieved January 12, 2012, from www.fdic.gov/consumers/consumer/news/cnwin1011/Win1011BW.pdf

Federal Deposit Insurance Corporation (FDIC Consumer News, Spring 2011). *Checking accounts: how to keep the costs down.* Retrieved January 5, 2012, from www.fdic.gov/consumers/consumer/news/cnspr11/Spr11BW.pdf

Federal Deposit Insurance Corporation (FDIC Consumer News, Winter 2009/2010). *Online banking, bill paying and shopping.* Retrieved January 12, 2012, from www.fdic.gov/consumers/consumer/news/cnwin0910/Winter0910BW.pdf

Federal Deposit Insurance Corporation (FDIC Consumer News, Spring 2009). *Shopping for a CD: be informed, be safe.* Retrieved January 10, 2012, from www.fdic.gov/consumers/consumer/news/cnspr09/shopping.html

Garman, E. and Forgue, R. (2010). *Personal Finance (10th ed.).* Mason, OH: South-Western Cengage Learning.

National Credit Union Administration (n.d.). *Is a credit union right for me?* Retrieved January 13, 2012, from www.mycreditunion.gov/about-credit-unions/Pages/Is-a-Credit-Union-Right-for-Me.aspx

Pritchard, J. (n.d.). *3 reasons not to use online bank accounts.* Retrieved January 12, 2012, from http://banking.about.com/od/savings/a/3onlinebankacct.htm

ORK STUDY

GRANTS

SCHOLARSHIPS

LOANS

CHAPTER OUTLINE

Financial Aid Defined

Options for Financial Aid

The Financial Aid Office

Applying for Financial Aid

Managing Your Student Loans

5 | Financial Aid Know-How

THE BIG PICTURE

Understanding and applying for financial aid is a process that many students will undertake as they seek their degrees. Chapter 5 addresses the financial aid maze, how to apply for it, and the myriad options available for student loans that best meet your financial and educational goals.

LEARNING OBJECTIVES

By the end of this chapter, you will achieve the following objectives:

▸ Define financial aid and explore the various options available for financial aid.

▸ Explain the importance of the financial aid office.

▸ Review FAFSA and other forms associated with applying for financial aid.

▸ Review the process of managing student loans.

▸ Discuss the consequences of defaulting on student loans.

CHAPTER 5 CASE IN POINT

Tori Marks is a senior in high school in a suburban town outside Seattle, WA. She has already been accepted to the school of her choice and will enroll in classes for the fall semester. Tori's parents, dual-income earners, both have good jobs, but they have found it difficult to save a substantial amount toward Tori's tuition and other expenses. They also have to consider paying for Tori's two younger siblings to attend college a few years down the line.

Tori is a good student who has applied for several scholarships in the hope that they will help defray some of her college expenses. Nonetheless, Tori and her parents realize the need for some outside financial help but are confused by all the financial aid options that may be available to them.

Imagine yourself to be in Tori's position. Thoughtfully and honestly answer the following questions:

▶ How much do you *really* know about receiving financial aid for college?

▶ Can you identify the many financial aid options you may have?

▶ Do you know what procedures and forms are associated with applying for financial aid?

▶ Have you built a relationship with the financial aid office at your school?

▶ Are you aware of the processes and procedures needed to properly manage your student loans and the consequences of not doing so?

FINANCIAL AID DEFINED

As you are all too aware, a college education is an expensive proposition and may represent your largest financial obligation in your lifetime other than purchasing a home. Despite seemingly endless skyrocketing costs, a college education is one of the best investments you can make in yourself.

If you are already enrolled in school, you well recognize this cold, hard fact. And unless you are fortunate enough to be in a financial situation where your tuition and other costs are covered, you have most likely sought out one or more options for financial aid.

Simply stated, **financial aid** is any form of financial assistance from any number of sources. These sources can include (but are not limited to) family members, different types of savings plans, and, in the case of college financial aid, grants, work study programs, scholarships, and student loans.

OPTIONS FOR FINANCIAL AID

Student financial aid is available from a wide variety of sources, including the federal government, individual states, colleges and universities, and numerous other public and private agencies and organizations. Whatever the source, all forms of college aid fall into four basic categories:

There are many options available for financial aid. Choose the ones that best fit your needs.

▶ **LOANS.** Funds that are borrowed and must be repaid with interest. As a general rule, educational loans have more favorable terms and interest rates than traditional consumer loans.

▶ **GRANTS.** Gift aid that does not have to be repaid and is generally awarded according to financial need.

▶ **WORK-STUDY.** The Federal Work-Study Program (FWS) is a federally funded source of financial assistance used to offset education costs. Students who qualify earn money by working on campus while attending school. The money does not have to be repaid.

▶ **SCHOLARSHIPS.** Offered by the school, local and community organizations, private institutions, and trusts, scholarships do not have to be repaid and are generally awarded based on specific criteria. (General Services Administration, 2011 [a]).

FEDERAL STUDENT LOANS

If you are among the hundreds of thousands of students who need financial assistance to fund a college education, the best place for you to start this process is with the federal government. While the thought of all that red tape may send shivers down your spine, the U.S. Department of Education has many programs and support structures in place to help make the whole financial aid maze understandable and manageable to the consumer. The added bonus is that these student aid programs offer lower interest rates (by design) and longer repayment plans (also by design) than private entities that also offer student loans.

Eligibility for federal student aid is based on financial need and several other factors. The financial aid administrator at the college or career school you plan to attend will determine your eligibility. To receive aid from one of the government's programs, you must meet the following requirements:

▶ Demonstrate financial need (except for certain loans).

▶ Have a high school diploma or a General Education Development (GED) certificate.

▶ Be enrolled or accepted for enrollment as a regular student working toward a degree or certificate in an eligible program.

▶ Be a U.S. citizen or eligible noncitizen.

▶ Have a valid Social Security Number.

▶ Register with the Selective Service if required.

▶ Maintain satisfactory academic progress once in school.

▶ Certify that you are not in default on a federal student loan and do not owe money on a federal student grant.

▶ Certify that you will use federal student aid only for educational purposes (U.S. Department of Education, 2011 [a]).

The federal government's loan programs allow undergraduate and graduate students to borrow money to cover their education expenses. Parents also may borrow to pay education expenses for dependent undergraduate students. A student is considered dependent if he or she is under 24 years of age, has no dependents, and is not married, a veteran, a graduate or professional degree student, or a ward of the court. Generally, loan amounts depend on the student's year in school, cost of attendance, and the amount of other aid received. Some loans are based on the student's financial need and others are not (U.S. Department of Education, 2011 [b]). There are five federal loans:

▶ **FEDERAL PERKINS LOAN.** A Federal Perkins Loan is a low-interest loan for both undergraduate and graduate students with exceptional financial need. Federal Perkins Loans are made through a school's financial aid office (known as **campus-based aid**). Your school is your lender, and the loan is made with government funds. You must repay this loan to your school.

Your school will either pay you directly (usually by check) or apply your loan to your school charges. You'll receive the loan in at least two payments during the academic year.

- **Campus-based aid.** Note that campus-based aid programs such as the Federal Perkins Loan provide a certain amount of funds for each participating school to administer each year. When the money for a program is gone, no more awards can be made from that program for that year. So make sure you apply for federal student aid as early as you can. Each school sets its own deadlines for campus-based funds, and those deadlines are usually earlier than the Department of Education's deadline for filing the *Free Application for Federal Student Aid* **(FAFSA)**. (Read more about FAFSA later in this chapter.)

- **Borrowing limits.** You can borrow up to $5,500 for each year of undergraduate study with the Federal Perkins Loan (the total you can borrow as an undergraduate is $27,500). For graduate studies, you can borrow up to $8,000 per year (the total you can borrow as a graduate is $60,000, which includes amounts borrowed as an undergraduate). The amount you receive depends on when you apply, your financial need, and the funding level at the school.

- **Other charges.** This type of loan has no other charges. However, if you skip a payment, if it's late, or if you make less than a full payment, you might have to pay a late charge plus any collection costs (U.S. Department of Education, 2009 [c]).

▶ **DIRECT STAFFORD LOANS.** Direct Stafford Loans, from the William D. Ford Federal Direct Loan (Direct Loan) Program, are low-interest loans for eligible students to help cover the cost of higher education at a four-year college or university, community college, or trade, career, or technical school. Eligible students borrow directly from the U.S. Department of Education at participating schools. Direct Stafford Loans include the following types of loans:

- **Direct Subsidized Loans**—Direct Subsidized Loans are for students with financial need. Your school will review the results of your *Free Application for Federal Student*

Aid (FAFSA) and determine the amount you can borrow. You are not charged interest while you're in school at least half-time and during **deferment** (a temporary suspension of loan payments for specific situations such as reenrollment in school, unemployment, or economic hardship) periods.

- **Direct Unsubsidized Loans**—You are not required to demonstrate financial need to receive a Direct Unsubsidized Loan. Like subsidized loans, your school will determine the amount you can borrow. Interest accrues (accumulates) on an unsubsidized loan from the time it's first paid out. You can pay the interest while you are in school and during grace periods and deferment or **forbearance** (a temporary postponement of payments, temporary ability to make smaller payments periods, or extend the time for making payments) or you can allow interest to accrue and be capitalized (that is, added to the principal amount of your loan). If you choose not to pay the interest as it accrues, this increases the total amount you have to repay because you will be charged interest on a higher principal amount.

- **Applying for a loan**. When you receive a Stafford Loan for the first time, you must complete a **Master Promissory Note (MPN)**. The MPN is a legal document in which you promise to repay your loan and any accrued interest and fees to the Department of Education. It also explains the terms and conditions of your loan. In most cases, one MPN can be used for loans that you receive over several years of study.

- **Borrowing limits**. Limits are placed on the maximum amount you are eligible to receive each academic year (annual loan limit) and in total (aggregate loan limits). The actual amount you can borrow each year depends on your year in school, whether you are a dependent or independent student, and other factors. Your school will determine what types of loans you are eligible for and how much you may borrow.

Depending on your financial need, you may be eligible to receive a subsidized loan for an amount up to the annual subsidized loan borrowing limit for your level of study. Note that effective for loans made for payment periods that begin on or after July 1, 2012, graduate and professional students are no longer eligible to receive subsidized loans. If you have education expenses that have not been met by subsidized loans and other aid, you may also receive an unsubsidized loan so long as you don't exceed the combined subsidized and unsubsidized annual loan limits.

- **Payment method.** You'll be paid through your school, generally in at least two installments. No installment may exceed one-half of your loan amount. Your school will use your loan money first to pay for tuition and fees, room and board, and other school charges. If any loan money remains, you'll receive the funds by check or other means, unless you give the school written authorization to hold the funds until later in the enrollment period.

  Generally, if you're a first-year undergraduate student *and* a first-time borrower, your school cannot disburse (distribute) your first payment until 30 days after the first day of your enrollment period.

- **Other charges**. In addition to interest, a loan fee is added to all Direct Subsidized and Unsubsidized Loans. The loan fee is a percentage of the amount of each loan you receive. For loans first disbursed on or after July 1, 2010, the loan origination fee is 1.0 percent. The loan origination fee is deducted proportionately from each loan disbursement. The specific loan origination fee you are charged will be reflected in a disclosure statement that is sent to you (U.S. Department of Education, 2011 [d]).

▶ **DIRECT PLUS LOANS FOR PARENTS.** Parents of dependent students may apply for a Direct PLUS Loan to help pay their child's education expenses as long as certain eligibility requirements are met:

- The parent borrower must be the student's biological or adoptive parent. In some cases, the student's stepparent may be eligible.

- The student must be a dependent student who is enrolled at least half-time at a school that participates in the Direct Loan Program. Generally, a student is considered dependent if he or she is under 24 years of age, has

5

no dependents, and is not married, a veteran, a graduate or professional degree student, or a ward of the court.

- The parent borrower must not have an adverse credit history (a credit check will be done). If the parent does not pass the credit check, the parent may still receive a loan if someone (such as a relative or friend who is able to pass the credit check) agrees to endorse the loan. The endorser promises to repay the loan if the parent fails to do so. The parent may also still receive a loan if he or she can demonstrate extenuating circumstances.

- The student and parent must be U.S. citizens or eligible noncitizens, must not be in default on any federal education loans or owe an overpayment on a federal education grant, and must meet other general eligibility requirements for the federal student aid programs.

- **Applying for a loan.** For a Direct PLUS Loan, the parent must complete a Direct PLUS Loan Application and Master Promissory Note (MPN).

- **Borrowing limits.** The annual limit on a PLUS Loan is equal to the student's cost of attendance minus any other financial aid the student receives. For example, if the cost of attendance is $6,000 and the student receives $4,000 in other financial aid, the student's parent can request up to $2,000.

- **Payment method.** The Department of Education will send the loan funds to the student's school. In most cases, the loan is disbursed in at least two installments, and no installment will be more than half the loan amount. The school will use the loan money first to pay the student's tuition, fees, room and board, and other school charges. If any loan funds remain, the parent will receive the amount as a check or other means, unless he or she authorizes the amount to be released to the student or transferred into the student's account at the school. Any remaining loan funds must be used for the student's education expenses.

- **Other charges.** The parent will pay a fee of 4 percent of the loan amount, deducted proportionately each time a loan disbursement is made (U.S. Department of Education, 2011 [e]).

▶ **DIRECT PLUS LOANS FOR GRADUATE AND PROFESSIONAL DEGREE STUDENTS.** Graduate and professional degree students can borrow a Direct PLUS Loan to help cover education expenses.

- **Applying for a loan.** For a PLUS Loan, you must complete a Direct PLUS Loan Application and Master Promissory Note (MPN).

- **Borrowing limits.** The maximum PLUS Loan amount you can borrow is your cost of attendance (determined by the school) minus any other financial assistance you will receive.

- **Other charges.** There is a fee of 4 percent of the loan amount, deducted proportionately each time a loan disbursement is made (U.S. Department of Education, 2011 [f]).

▶ **DIRECT CONSOLIDATION LOAN.** A Direct Consolidation Loan allows a borrower to consolidate (combine) multiple federal student loans into one loan. The result is a single monthly payment instead of multiple payments.

Make sure you carefully consider whether loan consolidation is the best option for you. While loan consolidation can simplify loan repayment and lower your monthly payment, it can also significantly increase the total cost of repaying your loans. Consolidation offers lower monthly payments by giving you up to 30 years to repay your loans. But, if you increase the length of your repayment period, you'll also make more payments and pay more in interest than you would otherwise. In fact, in some situations, consolidation can double your total interest expense. If you don't need monthly payment relief, you should compare the cost of repaying your unconsolidated loans against the cost of repaying a consolidation loan.

You should also take into account the impact of losing any borrower benefits offered under repayment plans for the original loans. Borrower benefits from your original loan, which may include interest rate discounts, principal rebates, or some loan-cancellation benefits, can significantly reduce the cost of repaying your loans. You may lose those benefits if you consolidate.

5

Once your loans are combined into a Direct Consolidation Loan, they cannot be removed. That's because the consolidated loans have been paid off and no longer exist. Take the time to study the pros and cons of consolidation before you submit your application.

GRANTS

The Department of Education offers a variety of federal grants to students attending four-year colleges or universities, community colleges, and career schools. Grants, unlike loans, are financial aid that does not have to be repaid. There are four types of federal grants:

▶ **FEDERAL PELL GRANT.** Pell Grants are awarded usually only to undergraduate students who have not earned a bachelor's or a professional degree. (In some cases, however, a student enrolled in a post-baccalaureate teacher certification program might receive a Pell Grant.) Pell Grants are considered a foundation of federal financial aid to which aid from other federal and nonfederal sources might be added.

- **Award amount.** The maximum Pell Grant award for the 2012–13 award year (July 1, 2012 to June 30, 2013) is $5,550. The amount you get, though, depends not only on your financial need but also on your costs to attend school, your status as a full-time or part-time student, and your plans to attend school for a full academic year or less. Once you have received a **Pell Grant** for 12 semesters, or the equivalent, you are no longer eligible for additional Pell Grants.

- **Payment method.** Your school can apply Pell Grant funds to your school costs, pay you directly (usually by check), or combine these methods. The school must tell you in writing how much your award will be and how and when you'll be paid. Schools must disburse funds at least once per term (semester, trimester, or quarter). Schools that do not use semesters, trimesters, or quarters must disburse funds at least twice per academic year (U.S. Department of Education, 2011 [g]).

▶ **FEDERAL SUPPLEMENTAL EDUCATIONAL OPPORTUNITY GRANT (FSEOG).** The Federal Supplemental Educational Opportunity Grant (FSEOG) program is for undergraduates with exceptional financial need. Pell Grant recipients with the lowest **expected family contributions (EFCs)** are considered first for an FSEOG. Just like Pell Grants, the FSEOG does not have to be repaid.

- **Award amount.** You can receive between $100 and $4,000 a year, depending on when you apply, your financial need, the funding at the school you're attending, and the policies of the financial aid office at your school.

- **Payment method.** If you're eligible, your school will credit your account, pay you directly (usually by check), or combine these methods. Your school must pay you at least once per term (semester, trimester, or quarter). Schools that do not use semesters, trimesters, or quarters must disburse funds at least twice per academic year (U.S. Department of Education, 2011 [h]).

▶ **IRAQ AND AFGHANISTAN SERVICE GRANT.** A student whose parent or guardian was a member of the U.S. Armed Forces and died as a result of service performed in Iraq or Afghanistan after September 11, 2001, may be eligible to receive the Iraq and Afghanistan Service Grant (U.S. Department of Education, 2011 [i]).

▶ **TEACHER EDUCATION ASSISTANCE FOR COLLEGE AND HIGHER EDUCATION (TEACH) GRANT PROGRAM.** Through the College Cost Reduction and Access Act of 2007, Congress created the Teacher Education Assistance for College and Higher Education (TEACH) Grant Program that provides grants of up to $4,000 per year to students who intend to teach in a public or private elementary or secondary school that serves students from low-income families. If you are interested in learning more about the TEACH Grant Program, you should contact the financial aid office at the college where you will be enrolled (U.S. Department of Education, 2011 [j]).

WORK-STUDY

Federal Work-Study (FWS), another type of campus-based aid, provides part-time jobs for undergraduate and graduate students with financial need, allowing them to earn money to help pay education expenses. The program encourages community service

5

work and work related to the recipient's course of study. More information about the Federal Work-Study program is available at the U.S. Department of Education's Federal Student Aid Web site at www.studentaid.ed.gov.

- **Payment method.** You'll be paid by the hour if you're an undergraduate. No FWS student may be paid by commission or fee. Your school must pay you directly (unless you indicate otherwise) and at least monthly. Wages for the program must equal at least the current federal minimum wage but might be higher, depending on the type of work you do and the skills required. The amount you earn can't exceed your total FWS award. When assigning work hours, your employer or financial aid administrator will consider your award amount, your class schedule, and your academic progress.

- **Job opportunities.** If you work on campus, you'll usually work for your school. If you work off campus, your employer will usually be a private nonprofit organization or a public agency, and the work performed must be in the public interest.

  Your school might have agreements with private for-profit employers for Federal Work-Study jobs. This type of job must be relevant to your course of study (to the maximum extent possible). If you attend a career school, there might be further restrictions on the jobs you can be assigned (U.S. Department of Education, 2009 [c]).

SCHOLARSHIPS

Many students assume that they have to be brilliant, athletically talented, or gifted musically to earn a scholarship for college. What they don't realize is that sometimes they just need to be persistent!

Be persistent in getting good grades. Many colleges award scholarships to students with significant financial need in the accepted applicant group—a grant that you don't need to repay—just for making the cut and getting admitted.

Good grades won't hurt if you hope to get a scholarship even if your family doesn't demonstrate financial need. When scholarships are awarded on the basis of academic merit, without regard for need, students who have worked hard and achieved results in high school will be the winners.

You should also be persistent in seeking out other scholarship sources. Sometimes all it takes to get a scholarship is to find out who in your area is offering them: your church, your employer, your parents' employers, and local civic organizations. You'll just need to fill out any required applications or attend interviews on time to be considered (U.S. Department of Education, n.d. [k]).

A word to the wise: Scholarships, like financial aid, do not require up-front fees. Legitimate companies will help guide you through the financial aid and college application process for a fee, but disreputable companies may ask you for money up front and provide nothing in return. Red flags to watch out for include the following:

- **A money-back guarantee to secure a scholarship.** Don't believe it. Unscrupulous companies attach conditions that make it impossible to get the refund.

- **Secret scholarships.** If a company claims to have inside knowledge of scholarship money, it's lying. Information on scholarships is freely available to the public. Ask your librarian or school counselor.

- **Telling students they've been selected as finalists for awards.** If a company asks for an up-front fee, head for the nearest exit.

- **Asking for a student's checking account to confirm eligibility.** If a company wants bank account information or your credit card number to confirm or reserve a scholarship, it's a scam.

- **Quoting a relatively small monthly or weekly fee.** Asking for authorization to debit your checking account for an unspecified length of time or any other ongoing fees are a sure sign of a scam.

- **Unsolicited offers.** Whether it's an e-mail, a phone call, or it arrives in your mailbox, if you didn't request the information, ignore the offer (General Services Administration, 2011).

5

5

> ### *success steps for avoiding scholarship scams*
>
> **RED FLAGS TO WATCH OUT FOR WHEN BEING OFFERED A SCHOLARSHIP ARE THE FOLLOWING:**
>
> - A money-back guarantee
> - Secret scholarships
> - Being selected as a finalist for an award
> - Asking for checking account information to confirm eligibility
> - Weekly or monthly fees
> - Unsolicited offers

PRIVATE LOANS

In addition to federal student aid, as a consumer, you also have the opportunity to explore private loans to finance your education. Private loans, sometimes referred to as alternative loans, are offered by private lenders and do not include the benefits and protections available with federal student loans.

Private companies may offer you loans and other forms of financial assistance for your education. They often use direct-mail marketing, telemarketing, television, radio, and online advertising to promote their products.

Private loans tend to have higher fees and interest rates than federal government loans. Private loans also do not offer the opportunities for cancellation or loan forgiveness that are available on many federal loan programs. So it makes good financial sense to exhaust your federal loan options (as well as grants and scholarships) before considering loans from any private companies.

How to Spot Deceptive Private Student Loan Practices

If you are considering a private student loan, it's important to know with whom you're doing business and the terms of the loan. The Federal Trade Commission and the U.S. Department of Education offer these tips to help you recognize questionable claims and practices related to private student loans:

- Some private lenders and their marketers use names, seals, logos, or other representations similar to those of government agencies to create the false or misleading impression that they are part of or affiliated with the federal government and its student loan programs.

- The Department of Education does not send advertisements or mailers or otherwise solicit consumers to borrow money. If you receive a student loan solicitation, it's not from the federal government.

- Don't let promotions or incentives like gift cards, credit cards, and sweepstakes prizes divert you from assessing whether the key terms of the loan are reasonable.

- Don't give out personal information on the phone, through the mail, or over the Internet unless you know with whom you are dealing. Private student lenders typically ask for your student account number—often your Social Security number (SSN) or personal identification number (PIN)—saying they need it to help determine your eligibility. However, scam artists who purport to be private student lenders can misuse this information, so provide it or other personal information only if you have confidence in the private student lender with whom you are dealing.

- Check out the track record of particular private student lenders with your state attorney general (www.naag.org), your local consumer protection agency (www.consumeraction.gov), and the Better Business Bureau (www.bbb.org) (Federal Trade Commission, 2008).

THE FINANCIAL AID OFFICE

One of your greatest allies when seeking any form of student financial aid comes from the financial aid office at your school. The relationship you have with this office should be ongoing because you will have questions about many things related to all facets of financial aid during your stay in school. In addition, if you plan to avail yourself of aid for the entire time you will be enrolled, you must reapply for that

Ryan Kelm/Shutterstock.com

The Financial Aid office at your school can assist you with all facets of receiving and repaying various forms of financial aid.

5

aid during each academic year. The financial office is well equipped to help you with that process.

Three of the best sources of information at your disposal are your school's financial aid office's Web site, the office's **financial aid administrator (FAA)**, and the staff at the office. A financial aid administrator is an individual who works at a college or career school and is responsible for preparing and communicating information on student loans, grants or scholarships, and employment programs. The FAA and staff help students apply for and receive student aid. The FAA is also capable of analyzing student needs and making professional judgment changes when necessary. The FAA (or office staff) can answer these types of questions for you:

- What financial aid can I apply for through my school and through my state education agency?
- What are the financial aid application deadlines at my school?
- How do I fill out the *Free Application for Federal Student Aid* (FAFSA)?
- Do I have to include my parents' information on the FAFSA?

- I went to a Web site that I thought was the FAFSA site, but it asked for my credit card number. Do I need to pay to fill out the FAFSA?
- What am I supposed to do with my **Student Aid Report (SAR)**?
- What is verification, what documents must I provide and when, and why was I chosen in the first place?
- When will I find out how much aid I've been awarded?
- What are all these different kinds of aid my school has awarded me?
- What if I'm not awarded enough money to pay for all my school-related expenses?

If you have any other questions or concerns about the financial aid process, contact the financial aid office at your school. The FAA and other professional staff members are there to help you, so use them to your fullest advantage. This office may also run programs or workshops for students to attend.

APPLYING FOR FINANCIAL AID

Like many other things in your life, applying for financial aid, either through the federal government or through a private entity, is something you will have to do as you pursue your education. However, the financially literate student understands that going through this process is the key to securing the biggest financial aid package possible.

THE FREE APPLICATION FOR FEDERAL STUDENT AID (FAFSA)

If you are seeking federal student aid in any fashion (loans, grants, or work study), the first and most important task at hand is filling out the *Free Application for Federal Student Aid* (FAFSA) form.

While the entire FAFSA process and the particulars of awarding federal student aid are beyond the scope of this book, Table 5-1 provides a summary of the steps involved in filing the FAFSA (also visit this book's companion Web site at www.cengagebrain.com for various forms and documents that support the FAFSA process).

FREE APPLICATION FOR FEDERAL STUDENT AID
July 1, 2011 — June 30, 2012

Step One (Student): For questions 1-31, leave blank any questions that do not apply to you (the student). OMB # 1845-0001

Your full name (**exactly as it appears on your Social Security card**)

1. Last name ☐☐☐☐☐☐☐☐☐☐☐☐☐☐☐☐☐☐☐

2. First name ☐☐☐☐☐☐☐☐☐☐☐☐☐☐☐

3. Middle initial ☐

Your mailing address

4. Number and street (include apt. number) ☐☐☐☐☐☐☐☐☐☐☐☐☐☐☐☐☐☐☐☐☐☐☐

5. City (and country if not U.S.) ☐☐☐☐☐☐☐☐☐☐☐☐☐☐☐☐☐☐

6. State ☐☐

7. ZIP code ☐☐☐☐☐

8. Your Social Security Number ☐☐☐ – ☐☐ – ☐☐☐☐

9. Your date of birth

MONTH	DAY	YEAR
☐☐	☐☐	1 9 ☐☐

10. Your permanent telephone number (☐☐☐) ☐☐☐ – ☐☐☐☐

Your driver's license number and driver's license state (if you have one)

11. Driver's license number ☐☐☐☐☐☐☐☐☐☐☐☐☐☐☐☐☐☐☐

12. Driver's license state ☐☐

13. Your e-mail address. If you provide your e-mail address, we will communicate with you electronically. For example, when your FAFSA has been processed, you will be notified by e-mail. Your e-mail address will also be shared with your state and the colleges listed on your FAFSA to allow them to communicate with you. If you prefer to be contacted by postal mail or do not have an e-mail address, please leave this field blank.

☐☐☐☐☐☐☐☐☐☐☐☐☐☐ @ ☐☐☐☐☐☐☐☐☐☐☐☐☐☐☐☐☐☐☐

14. Are you a U.S. citizen? Mark only one. **See Notes page 2.**

Yes, I am a U.S. citizen (U.S. national). **Skip to question 16.** ○ 1

No, but I am an eligible noncitizen. **Fill in question 15.** ○ 2

No, I am not a citizen or eligible noncitizen. **Skip to question 16.** ○ 3

15. Alien Registration Number A ☐☐☐☐☐☐☐☐

Report your marital status as of the date you sign your FAFSA.
If your marital status changes after you sign your FAFSA, you cannot change this information.

16. What is your marital status as of today?

I am single ○ 1   I am separated ○ 3

I am married/remarried ○ 2   I am divorced or widowed ○ 4

17. Month and year you were married, remarried, separated, divorced or widowed.

MONTH	YEAR
☐☐	☐☐☐☐

18. What is your state of legal residence? STATE ☐☐

19. Did you become a legal resident of this state before January 1, 2006?

Yes ○ 1   No ○ 2

20. If the answer to question 19 is "No," give month and year you became a legal resident.

MONTH	YEAR
☐☐	☐☐☐☐

21. Are you male or female?

Male ○ 1

Female ○ 2

22. **If female, skip to question 23.** Most male students must register with Selective Service to receive federal aid. If you are male, age 18-25 and not registered, fill in the circle and we will register you. **See Notes page 2.**

Register me ○ 1

23. Have you been convicted for the possession or sale of illegal drugs for an offense that occurred while you were receiving federal student aid (such as grants, loans or work-study)?
Answer "No" if you have never received federal student aid or if you have never had a drug conviction while receiving federal student aid. If you have a drug conviction for an offense that occurred while you were receiving federal student aid, answer "Yes," but complete and submit this application, and we will mail you a worksheet to help you determine if your conviction affects your eligibility for aid. If you are unsure how to answer this question, call 1-800-433-3243 for help.

No ○ 1

Yes ○ 3

Some states and colleges offer aid based on the level of schooling your parents completed.

24. Highest school your father completed   Middle school/Jr. high ○ 1   High school ○ 2   College or beyond ○ 3   Other/unknown ○ 4

25. Highest school your mother completed   Middle school/Jr. high ○ 1   High school ○ 2   College or beyond ○ 3   Other/unknown ○ 4

26. When you begin college in the 2011-2012 school year, what will be your high school completion status?

High school diploma. **Answer question 27.** .... ○ 1

General Educational Development (GED) certificate. **Skip to question 28.** .... ○ 2

Homeschooled. **Skip to question 28.** .... ○ 3

None of the above. **Skip to question 28.** .... ○ 4

U.S. Department of Education

Steps to Federal Student Aid
STEP 1 Get free information and help from a school counselor, the financial aid office at the college or trade school you plan to attend, or the U.S. Department of Education at www.studentaid.ed.gov or 1-800-4-FED-AID (1-800-433-3243). Free help is available any time during the application process. You should never have to pay for help.
STEP 2 Collect the documents needed to apply, including income tax returns and W-2 forms (and other records of income). A full list of what you need is at www.fafsa.gov and on this textbook's Web site at www.cengagebrain.com. If your tax return is not completed at the time you apply, then estimate the tax information, apply, and correct the information later.
STEP 3 Complete the FAFSA between Jan. 1, 2012, and June 30, 2013 (no exceptions to either date!). But apply as soon as possible after Jan. 1 to meet school and state aid deadlines. Apply online at FAFSA on the Web (the faster and easier way) by going to www.fafsa.gov. If you don't already have your PIN to electronically sign your FAFSA, you can get it when you complete the online FAFSA.
STEP 4 Within a few days, the U.S. Department of Education will send you your Student Aid Report (SAR)—the result of your FAFSA—by e-mail with a link to your electronic SAR or by mail if you completed a paper FAFSA. Review your SAR and, if necessary, make changes or corrections following the instructions in your SAR. Your complete, correct SAR will contain your Expected Family Contribution (EFC)—the number used to determine your federal student aid eligibility.
STEP 5 The college or trade school that you plan to attend might request additional information from you. Be sure to respond by any deadlines, or you might not receive federal student aid.
STEP 6 **All applicants:** The college or trade school will tell you how much aid you can get at that school. Contact the school's financial aid office if you have any questions about the aid being offered. **First-time applicants:** Review award letters from schools to compare amounts and types of aid being offered. Decide which school to attend based on a combination of (a) how well the school suits your needs and (b) its affordability after all aid is taken into account.

Table 5-1   Steps to Federal Student Aid (U.S. Department of Education, 2011 [I]).

MANAGING YOUR STUDENT LOANS

The next step in your financial aid journey is to manage the loan(s) you have been awarded. Just like other aspects of your financial life, you need to keep a careful watch on what is expected of you in respect to any loan you receive and the timing of events surrounding it.

5

There are two major phases to managing your student loans: while you are in school and when you graduate or leave school.

WHILE YOU ARE IN SCHOOL

While you are attending school, you need to be aware of several items as they pertain to your loan(s):

▶ **HOW THE LOANS ARE DISBURSED (PAID OUT).** Generally, your loan will cover a full academic year, and your school will make at least two disbursements to you, for example, at the beginning of each semester or quarter or at the beginning and midpoint of your academic year.

In most cases, your school will disburse your loan money by crediting it to your school account to pay tuition and fees, room and board, and other authorized charges. If the loan disbursement amount exceeds your school charges, the school will pay you the remaining balance of the disbursement directly by check or other means. Your school will notify you in writing each time they disburse part of your loan money and will provide information about how to cancel all or part of your disbursement if you find you no longer need the money. You will also receive a notice from your loan servicer confirming the disbursement. Read and then keep all correspondence received concerning your loan.

▶ **USING THE LOAN FOR EDUCATION EXPENSES.** You may use the loan money you receive only to pay for your education expenses at the school that is giving you the loan. Education expenses include school charges such as tuition, room and board, fees, and indirect expenses such as books, supplies, equipment, dependent child care expenses, transportation, and rental or purchase of a personal computer.

▶ **ENROLLMENT STATUS AND OTHER CHANGES.** It's important to keep your loan servicer informed of any changes in your status so that your loan information is up to date. This is your responsibility.

You must notify the loan servicer if you do any of the following:

• Change your local address, permanent address, or telephone number.

• Change your name (for example, maiden name to married name).

- Do not enroll at least half-time for the loan period certified by the school.
- Do not enroll at the school that certified your loan.
- Stop attending school or drop below half-time enrollment.
- Transfer from one school to another school.
- Graduate.

Until you graduate or leave school, you must also keep your school's financial aid office informed of these changes.

A scheduled break in enrollment, such as the summer session at many traditional four-year schools, is not considered an interruption in your enrollment if you are planning to return to school during the next regularly scheduled enrollment period.

When you graduate, drop below half-time, or withdraw from your academic program, you will receive a six-month **grace period** for your Direct Subsidized and Unsubsidized Loans. Once your grace period ends, you must begin repaying your loan(s).

▶ **PAYING INTEREST WHILE IN SCHOOL.** You may choose to pay interest on your Direct Unsubsidized or Direct PLUS loans while you are in school. If you choose not to pay the interest while you're in school, it will be added to the unpaid principal amount of your loan. This is called **capitalization**, and it can substantially increase the amount you repay, especially if you are receiving multiple loans for a multiyear program. Capitalization increases the unpaid principal balance of your loan, and you will be charged interest on the increased principal amount.

It will save you money in the long run if you pay the interest as it accrues on your loan while you're in school or during the grace period. This is also true if you pay any interest that accrues during periods of deferment or forbearance after you leave school (U.S. Department of Education, 2011 [m]).

WHEN YOU GRADUATE OR LEAVE SCHOOL

Here's what you need to do when you are no longer in school:

▶ **LEAVING SCHOOL: GRADUATING, WITHDRAWING, OR DROPPING BELOW HALF-TIME.** Once you are no longer enrolled at least half-time in an eligible program or upon graduation, you'll receive a six-month grace period on your Direct Subsidized and Unsubsidized Loans during which you are not required to make loan payments. You must begin repayment at the end of your grace period.

Make sure that both your school and loan servicer know that you are no longer enrolled. If you don't begin making payments when required, you could lose repayment incentives you may have received or even go into default.

Your school is required to ensure that you receive exit counseling, which is required before you withdraw, graduate, or drop below half-time attendance (even if you plan to transfer to another school). The program is designed to help you understand your rights and responsibilities as a student loan borrower, and it provides useful tips and information to help you manage your loans. Check with your school to see how exit counseling is conducted because some schools allow you to complete this requirement online.

If you reenroll in school at least half-time before the end of your six-month grace period, you will receive the full six-month grace period when you stop attending school or drop below half-time enrollment.

▶ **CHOOSING A REPAYMENT PLAN.** You'll have the choice of several repayment plans, and the loan servicer will notify you of the date your first payment is due. If you do not choose a repayment plan, you will be placed on the standard repayment plan. Most Direct Loan borrowers choose to stay with the standard repayment plan, but other options are available for borrowers who may need more time to repay or who need to make lower payments at the beginning of the repayment period.

▶ **CONSOLIDATION.** If you have multiple federal education loans, you can consolidate them into a single Direct Consolidation Loan. This may simplify repayment if you are currently making separate loan payments to different loan holders because you'll only have one monthly payment to make. As you learned earlier, there may be tradeoffs, so you'll want to learn about the advantages and possible disadvantages before you decide whether to consolidate.

TROUBLE MAKING PAYMENTS

If you're having trouble making payments on your loans, contact your loan servicer as soon as possible to discuss options that may help you.

Options include the following:

- **Changing repayment plans.** Give careful consideration as to what type of repayment plan will work best for you under the circumstances.

- **Deferment.** If you meet certain requirements (for example, if you are unable to find full-time employment or are experiencing an economic hardship), a deferment allows you to temporarily stop making payments on your loan.

- **Forbearance.** Consider forbearance if you don't meet the eligibility requirements for a deferment but are temporarily unable to make your loan payments. Forbearance allows you to temporarily stop making payments on your loan, temporarily make smaller payments, or extend the time for making payments.

If you stop making payments and don't get a deferment or forbearance, your loan could go into default, which has serious consequences. Your loan first becomes delinquent if your monthly payment is not received by the due date. If you fail to make a payment, your Direct Loan servicer will send you a reminder that your payment is late. If your account remains delinquent, your loan servicer will send you warning notices reminding you of your obligation to repay your loans and the consequences of default.

If you are delinquent on your loan payments, contact your loan servicer immediately to find out how to bring your account current. Note that late fees may be added, and your delinquency will be reported to one or more national consumer reporting agencies (credit bureaus), but bringing your account up to date is much better than remaining delinquent on your payments and going into default.

CONSEQUENCES OF DEFAULTING ON YOUR LOAN

Default occurs when you become 270 days past due (delinquent) in making a payment on your loan(s). The consequences of default can be severe:

- The entire unpaid balance of your loan and accrued interest becomes due and payable immediately.

- You lose eligibility for deferment.

- You lose eligibility for additional federal student financial aid.

- Your account is assigned to a collection agency.

- The default will be reported as delinquent to credit bureaus, damaging your credit rating.
- The federal government can take all or part of your federal tax refund.
- Late fees, additional interest, court costs, collection fees, attorney's fees, and other costs incurred in collecting your loan will increase your loan debt.
- Your employer (at the request of the federal government) can garnish part of your wages and send them to the government.
- The federal government can take legal action against you (U.S. Department of Education, 2010 [n]).

The financially literate student knows, above all, *not* to default on his student loans!

CASE IN POINT REVISITED

In the Case in Point presented at the beginning of this chapter, Tori Marks had been accepted to the college of her choice and was preparing to start classes during the fall semester. Despite well-intended efforts by her parents to save sufficient money to fund her education, Tori needed financial aid but was unsure and confused by the many steps involved in securing student loans or other financing.

On the advice of her guidance counselor at her high school, Tori and her parents contacted the financial aid office at her college to get advice on her options for financial aid, including direct federal student loans and work-study programs. In addition, the financial aid office offered guidance as to how to apply for these programs and how to fill out the required forms.

CHAPTER SUMMARY

Chapter 5 introduced you to many facets of federal and private student aid. You learned about the five types of federal student loans, the four federal grant programs, and how federal work-study programs function. You also learned about the importance of your school's financial aid office and the steps to filing the *Free Application for Federal Student Aid* (FAFSA) form. Finally, you learned how to manage your student loans and the consequences of defaulting on those loans.

POINTS TO KEEP IN MIND

▶ Federal student aid includes grants, work study, and student loans.

▶ Scholarships are a form of financial aid, but the federal government does not fund them.

▶ There are five federal student loans: Federal Perkins Loans, Direct Stafford Loans, Direct PLUS Loan for Parents, Direct PLUS Loans for Graduate and Professional Degree Students, and Direct Consolidation Loans.

▶ All federal and private student loans must be repaid with interest.

▶ There are four types of federal grants: the Federal Pell Grant, the Federal Supplemental Educational Opportunity Grant, the Iraq and Afghanistan Service Grant, and the Teacher Education Assistance for College and Higher Education (TEACH) Grant. Unlike federal student loans, grants do not have to be repaid.

▶ Federal Work-Study (FWS) provides part-time jobs for undergraduate and graduate students with financial need, allowing them to earn money to help pay education expenses.

▶ Private loans, sometimes referred to as alternative loans, are offered by private lenders and do not include the benefits and protections available with federal student loans.

▶ Your school's financial aid office is an important resource if you have any form of financial aid.

▶ The *Free Application for Federal Student Aid* (FAFSA) form must be filled out if you are seeking any type of federal financial aid.

▶ It is important to manage your student loans while you are in school and after you graduate.

> Student loan repayment starts six months after you graduate.

> Defaulting on your student loans carries dire financial consequences.

CRITICAL THINKING QUESTIONS

1. Why is it advisable to start paying off the interest on your student loans while you are still in school?

2. There are several advantages to receiving a federal student loan versus a private student loan. List as many as you can.

3. Aside from the financial aid office, how might you go about researching scholarship opportunities on your own?

4. If you were in the process of repaying your student loans, would you take advantage of loan consolidation? Why or why not?

5. Why do you think exit counseling is so important upon graduating or leaving school?

apply it!

 Activity #1: Your School's Financial Aid Web Site

GOAL: Gain a greater understanding of the services available at your school's Financial Aid Web site.

STEP 1: Log on to your school's student portal and click on the "Financial Aid" tab or link.

STEP 2: Write down 10 items about your financial aid office that you did not know previously and how this information will be helpful to you during your enrollment.

STEP 3: Be prepared to share your information with the class.

CHECK YOUR UNDERSTANDING

Visit www.cengagebrain.com to see how well you have mastered the material in Chapter 5.

REFERENCES

Federal Trade Commission (2008). FTC Facts for Consumers. *Student loans: avoiding deceptive offers.* Retrieved February 7, 2012, from https://studentaid.ed.gov/students/attachments/siteresources/loansAvoidDecep.pdf

General Services Administration (2011 [a]). *Consumer Action Handbook: Financing Your Education.* Retrieved January 15, 2012, from www.usa.gov/topics/consumer/consumer-action-handbook.pdf

U.S. Department of Education (2011 [b]). *About us.* Retrieved February 6, 2012, from http://studentaid.ed.gov/PORTALSWebApp/students/english/aboutus.jsp

U.S. Department of Education (2009 [c]). *Campus-based aid.* Retrieved February 6, 2012, from http://studentaid.ed.gov/PORTALSWebApp/students/english/campusaid.jsp#03

U.S. Department of Education (2011 [f]). *Direct PLUS loans for graduate and professional degree programs.* Retrieved February 6, 2012, from http://studentaid.ed.gov/PORTALSWebApp/students/english/PlusLoansGradProfstudents.jsp

U.S. Department of Education (2011 [e]). *Direct PLUS loans for parents.* Retrieved February 6, 2012, from http://studentaid.ed.gov/PORTALSWebApp/students/english/parentloans.jsp

U.S. Department of Education (2011 [d]). *Direct Stafford loans.* Retrieved February 6, 2012, from http://studentaid.ed.gov/PORTALSWebApp/students/english/studentloans.jsp

U.S. Department of Education (2010 [n]). *Entrance counseling guide for direct loan borrowers.* Retrieved February 8, 2012, from http://direct.ed.gov/pubs/entrcounselguide.pdf

U.S. Department of Education (2011 [g]). *Federal Pell grants.* Retrieved February 6, 2012, from http://studentaid.ed.gov/PORTALSWebApp/students/english/PellGrants.jsp

5

U.S. Department of Education (2011 [h]). *Federal supplemental educational opportunity grant.* Retrieved February 6, 2012, from http://studentaid.ed.gov/PORTALSWebApp/students/english/FSEOG.jsp

U.S. Department of Education (2011 [i]). *Iraq and Afghanistan service grant.* Retrieved February 6, 2012, from http://studentaid.ed.gov/PORTALSWebApp/students/english/IraqAfghanServiceGrant.jsp

U.S. Department of Education (2011 [l]). *Steps to federal student aid.* Retrieved February 8, 2012, from http://studentaid.ed.gov/students/attachments/siteresources/12-13_Guide.pdf

U.S. Department of Education (2011 [a]). *Student aid eligibility.* Retrieved February 6, 2012, from http://studentaid.ed.gov/PORTALSWebApp/students/english/aideligibility.jsp

U.S. Department of Education (2011[j]). *TEACH grant program.* Retrieved February 6, 2012, from http://studentaid.ed.gov/PORTALSWebApp/students/english/TEACH.jsp

U.S. Department of Education (n.d. [k]). *What does it take to get a scholarship?* Retrieved January 31, 2012, from https://studentaid2.ed.gov/getmoney/pay_for_college/scholarship_get.html

U.S. Department of Education (2011 [m]). *While you're in school.* Retrieved February 8, 2012, from www.direct.ed.gov/inschool.html

micro10x/Shutterstock.com

CHAPTER OUTLINE

Taxes: Obligations and Responsibilities for Paying Them

Tax-Reporting Components

Electronic Tax Return Preparation and Transmission

Consequences of Not Paying Taxes

6 Understanding Taxes

THE BIG PICTURE

Having to file personal taxes is another sign of adulthood and an important part of becoming financially literate. Chapter 6 identifies your obligations and responsibilities as a taxpayer, tax-reporting components, electronic tax preparation and transmission, and the consequences of not paying taxes.

By the end of this chapter, students will achieve the following objectives:

▶ Describe your obligations and responsibilities for paying taxes.

▶ Identify the components of tax reporting.

▶ Describe the mechanics of electronic tax return preparation and transmission.

▶ Explain the consequences of not paying taxes.

6

CHAPTER 6 CASE IN POINT

Spencer Burns is a full-time student at a school in northern Massachusetts. In addition to his studies, Spencer works part-time at a big box store in the town where his college is located. Having filled out a Form W-4 (Employee's Withholding Allowance Certificate) when he first started to work, Spencer knew that taxes were taken out of his paycheck each pay period, but he wasn't really sure for what reason.

Right after the first of the year, Spencer received a W-2, Wage and Tax Statement form, from his employer showing how much he had earned the previous year and the amount of income and payroll taxes he paid during that time. Unsure of what he should do with that information, Spencer put the form in a drawer and promptly forgot about it.

Imagine yourself in Spencer's place. Thoughtfully and honestly answer the following questions:

▶ Do you understand your personal obligations for filing taxes and your responsibilities for doing so?

▶ Can you identify the types of taxes you may be required to pay?

▶ Are you aware that there are different ways of filing your taxes?

▶ Do you know the consequences of not paying your taxes?

TAXES: OBLIGATIONS AND RESPONSIBILITIES FOR PAYING THEM

Even if you have never worked before, you have been paying tax somewhere, on something—gasoline, soda, clothing, and textbooks, to name a few. Taxes provide revenue for federal, local, and state governments to fund essential services—defense, highways, police, a justice system—that benefit all citizens who could not provide such services very effectively for themselves. Taxes also fund programs and services that benefit only certain citizens, for

John T Takai/Shutterstock.com

Paying your taxes on "Tax Day" is an inevitability for the vast majority of citizens.

6

example, health, welfare, and social services, job training, schools, and parks.

Article 1 of the United States Constitution grants the U.S. government the power to establish and collect taxes. Congress delegated to the **Internal Revenue Service (IRS)** the responsibility of administering and enforcing the **Internal Revenue Code**.

Taxes reduce taxpayers' income. As a result, taxpayers have less for personal goods and services, savings, and investments. The more services the government provides, the more taxpayers have to pay for them. Whenever new **public goods and services** are proposed that require new taxes, taxpayers must decide whether the additional benefits are worth the reduction in income.

Some public goods and services include the following:

▶ Highways
▶ National defense
▶ Police and fire protection
▶ Public schools
▶ Bank regulations
▶ Job training
▶ Libraries
▶ Air traffic controllers
▶ Subsidized school lunches
▶ Drug rehabilitation programs
▶ Scientific research

The U.S. income tax system is built on the idea of **voluntary compliance**, meaning yielding to a request or demand, in this case, the federal government. Compliance is voluntary when taxpayers declare all of their income. Taxpayers also voluntarily comply through obtaining forms and instructions, providing complete and correct information, and filing their income tax returns on time.

When people don't report their earnings, they are participating in an **underground economy**. Examples of an underground economy include illegal activities such as gambling and legal activities such as yardwork or babysitting. Because these types of income are often unreported, they are not taxed (Internal Revenue Service, n.d. [a]).

TAX-REPORTING COMPONENTS

If you have income from a job or savings, you probably have to file both a federal and a state tax return. That does not necessarily mean you will have to pay additional taxes—depending on your age and your overall income, you may well get a **refund** from your state and/or federal government the year following the year in which you filed (for example, getting a refund in 2013 on taxes paid in 2012).

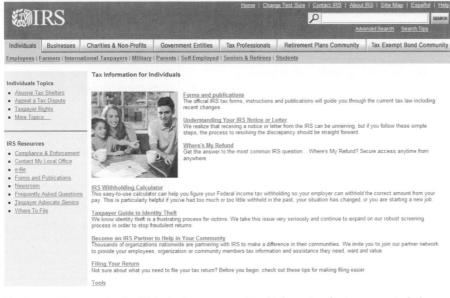

Internal Revenue Service

The Internal Revenue Service Web site houses a wealth of information for taxpayers, including various forms and instructions needed to file a return.

Each level of government—federal, state, and local—raises money through taxation of its citizens. Each level of government makes its own decisions about how and what to tax and how to spend the money. Although most federal revenue comes from **income taxes**, state and local revenues may come from three tax sources: **transaction taxes**, which are on the sale of goods and services; income taxes, which come from taxes on earned and unearned income; and **property taxes**, which come from taxes on property. See Table 6-1 for a further explanation of these taxes.

REVENUE SOURCES FOR STATE AND LOCAL GOVERNMENTS			
Type of Tax	**Definition**	**Examples**	**Revenues Support**
Transaction Taxes	Taxes on economic transactions, such as the sale of goods and services. These can be based on a set of percentages of the sales value (sales taxes), or they can be a set amount on physical quantities ("per unit"—gasoline taxes).	Retail sales taxes Excise taxes on vehicles, boats, gasoline, and tobacco "Value added" taxes imposed on goods at each stage of processing Restaurant and hotel taxes	State and local services, such as education, welfare, Medicaid, police, employment services, parks, fish and wildlife Gasoline taxes are often earmarked for state highway construction and maintenance.

Table 6-1   Revenue Sources for State and Local Governments (**Internal Revenue Service, n.d. [b]**) *continued*

REVENUE SOURCES FOR STATE AND LOCAL GOVERNMENTS			
Type of Tax	**Definition**	**Examples**	**Revenues Support**
Income Taxes	Taxes on income, both earned (salaries, wages, tips, commissions) and unearned (interest, dividends). Income taxes can be levied on individuals (personal income taxes) and businesses (business and corporate income taxes).	Federal, state, or local withholding taxes Taxes on interest or dividend payments Taxes on awards or prizes Taxes on profits and earnings in businesses	Increasingly supplementing or taking the place of some sales taxes to support state expenses Beginning to be used on the local level as well, largely to support education and welfare programs
Property Taxes	Taxes on personal and business property	Taxes on property, especially real estate (land and buildings), and boats, recreational vehicles, business inventories, or stocks and bonds ("intangibles")	Traditional source of funding for schools and local services (police, fire, libraries, parks, water, and sanitation)

Table 6-1 *continued*

PAYROLL TAX AND FEDERAL INCOME TAX WITHHOLDING

Income taxes are collected on a pay-as-you-earn basis. This means that employers withhold taxes from every paycheck and send the money to the IRS on the employee's behalf. At the year's end, this amount should be roughly equal to one's **tax liability**, or your total tax bill for the year. If you paid too much tax during the previous calendar year, you will receive a refund from the federal government, your state government, or perhaps both. If you did not pay sufficient tax during that time, you will owe monies to one or both entities.

Tax withholding benefits both taxpayers and the government. Without withholding, many would find it difficult to save enough money to pay their income taxes all at once. Government services might be disrupted and unreliable without continuous funding.

Tax deductions, **exemptions**, and **tax credits** may lower your tax liability. The government allows this special tax treatment to support or encourage behaviors, spending patterns, and lifestyles considered desirable (read more about tax deductions, exemptions, and tax credits later in this chapter).

Payroll taxes consist of two different types of taxes:

▶ **SOCIAL SECURITY TAX.** This is also known as the Federal Insurance Contributions Act (FICA) and it is displayed on paycheck stubs as FICA. Social Security taxes provide benefits for retired workers and their dependents and for disabled workers and their dependents. Social Security taxes comprise 4.2 percent of your **gross income**, or the amount paid to you before any taxes or other contributions are deducted.

▶ **MEDICARE TAX.** This tax is used to provide medical benefits for certain individuals when they reach age 65. Workers, retired workers, and the spouses of workers and retired workers are eligible to received Medicare benefits upon reaching age 65. Medicare tax comprises 1.45 percent of your gross income.

Federal income taxes are used to provide for national programs such as defense, community development, foreign affairs, law enforcement, and interest on the national debt. Employees complete **Form W-4, Employee's Withholding Allowance Certificate** when they begin work so that employers know how much income tax to withhold from their employees' pay. (Visit this textbook's Web site on www.cengagebrain.com for a copy of Form W-4.) (Internal Revenue Service, n.d. [d]).

Table 6-2, Table 6-3, and Table 6-4 show examples of paycheck stubs that show how different taxes are withheld. The employees shown here work in different states. Note that paycheck stubs can also show employees' contributions for insurance and savings programs.

EXAMPLE 1—NEW YORK STATE					
Earnings	Hours	Amount	Deduction	Current	Year-to-Date
Regular	70.00	846.16	FICA Tax	69.06	494.17
Overtime	14.75	267.57	Medicare Tax	16.15	115.58
Total	84.75	1,113.73	Federal Tax	116.17	880.89
			NY State Tax	52.40	347.68
			NY City Tax	27.05	183.34
			Disability	1.20	9.60
			Long-Term Disability	1.00	
Year-to-Date Gross		7,970.53	Total	283.03	
			Net Pay	830.70	

Table 6-2 New York State Paycheck Stub

EXAMPLE 2—WISCONSIN						
Earnings	Hours	Amount	YTD	Deduction	Amount	YTD
Regular	40.00	554.00	7,645.20	Federal W/H	72.95	1,054.81
Overtime	6.00	124.65	415.50	FICA	42.08	545.80
Holiday	.00	.00	271.60	Medicare	9.84	127.65
Sick Pay	.00	.00	110.80	E.I.C.	.00	3.05
Bonus	.00	.00	249.32	WI State W/H	42.34	505.83
Vacation	.00	.00	110.80	Health Insurance	60.00	480.00
				Credit Union	100.00	1,500.00
Gross Earnings		678.65	8,803.22	Total Deductions	327.21	4,217.14
Net Earnings		351.44		Allocated Tips	.00	128.53

Table 6-3   Wisconsin Paycheck Stub

EXAMPLE 3—INDIANA						
Earnings	Hrs/Unit	Current Amount	Year-to-Date	Deduction	Current Amount	Year-to-Date
Salary	75.00	1,007.31	23,961.12	FICA	62.45	1,576.94
Overtime 1		0.00	0.00	Federal W/H	154.16	3,823.59
Overtime 2		0.00	0.00	Indiana	34.25	864.89
Misc. #3		0.00	1,475.00	Monroe Co.	10.07	242.35
				Medicare	14.61	368.83
26,190.00 Pay Rate	1,007.31 Current Earnings	275.54 Current Deductions	731.77 Net Pay	25,436.12 YTD Earnings	6,876.60 YTD Deductions	18,559.52 YTD Deductions

Table 6-4   Indiana Paycheck Stub **(Internal Revenue Service, (n.d. [c]).**

WAGE AND TIP INCOME

As you noted in the Case In Point at the beginning of this chapter, Spencer Burns received a W-2, Wage and Tax Statement, from his employer by January 31 after the end of the current tax year, as required by law. (Visit this textbook's Web site on www.cengagebrain.com for a copy of Form W-2.) The W-2 contains the following information:

▶ **SALARY.** This is compensation received by an employee for services performed. A salary is a fixed sum paid for a specific period of time worked, such as weekly or monthly.

▶ **WAGES.** Wages are compensation received by employees for services performed. Usually, wages are computed by multiplying an hourly rate by the number of hours worked.

▶ **COMMISSION.** Like salaries and wages, commissions are compensation received by an employee for services performed. Commissions are paid based on a percentage of sales made or a fixed amount per sale.

▶ **BONUS.** A bonus is compensation received by an employee for services performed. A bonus is given in addition to an employee's usual compensation.

▶ **TIP INCOME.** Money and goods received for services performed by food servers, baggage handlers, babysitters, hairdressers, and others. Tips go beyond the stated amount of the bill and are given voluntarily.

Note the following important information about wages, salaries, bonuses, and tips:

- They may be in the form of cash, goods and services, awards, or taxable benefits.
- They are taxable and need to be reported on the taxpayer's individual income tax return.
- They are reported on Form W-2, Wage and Tax Statement.

So that you don't end up in the tax doghouse, remember that *all* wages, salaries, bonuses, commissions, and tips are taxable, even if they are not reported on Form W-2 (Internal Revenue Service, n.d. [e]).

INTEREST INCOME

As you learned earlier, interest is the charge for use of borrowed money. A common (and safe) way to earn interest income is to deposit funds in a financial institution such as a bank or credit union. Most interest income is taxable—that is, it is subject to income tax.

▶ **Tax-exempt interest income** is not subject to income tax and is earned on funds loaned to states, cities, counties, or the District of Columbia.

▶ **Taxable interest income** is reported on Form 1099-INT, Interest Income. All taxable interest income is reported on the taxpayer's return, even if it is not reported on Form 1099-INT. (For a copy of the form, visit this textbook's Web site on www.cengagelearning.com.) (Internal Revenue Service, n.d. [f]).

FILING STATUS

Another critical piece to understanding taxes is determining your **filing status**. Filing status determines the rate at which income is taxed. Some taxpayers can qualify for more than one filing status. Usually, taxpayers choose the filing status that results in the lowest tax.

There are five filing statuses:

▶ **SINGLE.** Taxpayers use the **single filing status** if, on the last day of the year, they had one of the following as their marital status:

- Never married

- Legally separated under a decree of divorce or separate maintenance

- Widowed before January 1 of that year, were not remarried, and have no dependents

▶ **MARRIED FILING JOINTLY.** Taxpayers may use the **married filing jointly status** if they are married and both agree to file a joint return. This status includes the following:

- Taxpayers who live together in a common-law marriage recognized by the state where the marriage began (Common-law states are Alabama, Colorado, District of Columbia, Iowa, Kansas, Montana, Oklahoma, Pennsylvania, Rhode Island, South Carolina, and Texas.)

- Taxpayers who live apart but are not legally separated

- Taxpayers whose spouses died during the year and who have not remarried

Both husband and wife must sign the income tax return. Special rules apply when a spouse cannot sign the tax return because of death, illness, or absence. Both husband and wife are responsible for any tax owed. The lowest tax rates apply to the married filing jointly filing status.

▶ **MARRIED FILING SEPARATELY.** Married taxpayers may choose to file separately under the **married filing separately filing status.** Each spouse prepares a separate tax return that reports his or her individual income and deductions. Tax rates are highest for the married filing separately filing status. Some taxpayers choose the married filing separately filing status so that one spouse will not be responsible for the other spouse's tax liability.

▶ **HEAD OF HOUSEHOLD.** Tax rates for head of household are lower than those for single taxpayers. In general, taxpayers use **head of household filing status** if both of the following apply:

- They are unmarried or considered unmarried as of the end of the year.

- They provide more than half the cost of keeping up a home for a qualified person for more than half of the year. (Dependent parents do **not** have to live with the taxpayer.) Keeping up a home includes rent, mortgage interest, taxes, insurance, repairs, utilities, paying for domestic help, and food eaten in the home.

▶ **QUALIFYING WIDOW(ER) WITH DEPENDENT CHILD.** Widows and widowers with one or more dependent children may be able to use the **qualifying widow(er) with dependent child filing status**. Tax rates for a qualifying widow(er) with a dependent child and for married filing jointly are the same. They are the lowest tax rates and usually result in the lowest total tax.

The five filing statuses are listed in order of lowest to highest tax rates:

- Married filing jointly
- Qualifying widow(er) with dependent child (Married filing jointly filing status and qualifying widow(er) with dependent child filing status have the same tax rates.)
- Head of household
- Single
- Married filing separately

EXEMPTIONS AND DEPENDENTS

Along with making sure you file a tax return with the lowest possible tax rate for your personal situation, you will also want to claim as many tax **exemptions** as you are allowed by law.

A tax exemption is the amount that taxpayers can claim for themselves, their spouses, and eligible dependents. There are two types of exemptions—**personal exemptions** and **dependency exemptions**. Each exemption reduces the taxpayer's income subject to tax. While each is worth the same amount (in 2011, for example, the **exemption amount** was $3,700), different rules apply to each type.

Only one exemption can be claimed per person, and an exemption for a particular person cannot be claimed on more than one tax return. So if you are a dependent of your parents and they claim you as a dependent on their tax form, you cannot file for an exemption on your tax form (assuming that you have income that must be reported).

Table 6-5 provides an overview of the rules for claiming an exemption for a dependent. Dependents fall into two categories: qualifying child and qualifying relative.

RULES FOR CLAIMING AN EXEMPTION FOR A DEPENDENT
• You cannot claim any dependents if you, or your spouse if filing jointly, could be claimed as a dependent by another taxpayer.
• You cannot claim a married person who files a joint return as a dependent unless that joint return is only a claim for a refund and there would be no tax liability for either spouse on separate returns.
• You cannot claim a person as a dependent unless that person is a U.S. citizen, U.S. resident alien, U.S. national, or a resident of Canada or Mexico for some part of the year.
• You cannot claim a person as a dependent unless that person is your qualifying child or qualifying relative.

Qualifying Child Rules	Qualifying Relative Rules
• The child must be your son, daughter, stepchild, eligible foster child, brother, sister, half brother, half sister, stepbrother, stepsister, or a descendent of any of them. • The child must be (a) under age 19 at the end of the year and younger than you (or your spouse if filing jointly), (b) under age 24 at the end of the year, a full-time student, and younger than you (or your spouse if filing jointly), or (c) any age permanently and totally disabled.	• The person cannot be your qualifying child or the qualifying child of anyone else. • The person either (a) must be related to you in one of the ways listed under Relatives who do not have to live with you, or (b) must live with you all year as a member of your household.

Table 6-5   Rules for Claiming an Exemption for a Dependent (**Internal Revenue Service, n.d. [g]**). *continued*

Qualifying Child Rules	Qualifying Relative Rules
• The child must have lived with you for more than half of the year. • The child must not have provided more than half of his or her own support for the year. • The child is not filing a joint return for the year. • If the child meets the rules to be a qualifying child of more than one person, only one person can actually treat the child as a qualifying child.	• The person's gross income for the year must be less than $3,700. • You must provide more than half of the person's total support for the year.

Table 6-5 *continued*

STANDARD DEDUCTION

Like exemptions, a **standard deduction** reduces the income subject to tax. The amount of the standard deduction depends on the following:

- The filing status
- The age of the taxpayer and spouse
- Whether the taxpayer or spouse is blind
- Whether the taxpayer can be claimed as a dependent on another taxpayer's return.

For most taxpayers, the standard deduction is based on filing status. Table 6-6 shows the standard deduction amounts for 2011 based on filing status.

Some taxpayers will itemize deductions. When their itemized deductions are greater than the standard deduction, they use the itemized deductions instead of the standard deduction. For the purposes of this book, we will focus only on the standard deduction.

2011 Standard Deduction	
Single	$ 5,800
Head of household	$ 8,500
Married filing jointly	$11,600
Qualifying widow(er) with dependent child	$11,600
Married filing separately	$ 5,800

Table 6-6 2011 Standard Deduction Amounts

Review the tax and credits section of the tax return for Brian and Sylvia Lyons (see Figure 6-1). Brian and Sylvia are married and file a joint return, using IRS Form 1040A, U.S. Individual Income Tax Return. (Visit this textbook's Web site on www.cengagebrain.com for a copy of this form.) They have three dependent children.

- The **adjusted gross income** is $63,825. Adjusted gross income is total income reduced by certain amounts, such as for an IRA or student loan interest (Line 38).
- The standard deduction is $11,600 (Line 40).
- The standard deduction ($11,600) subtracted from the adjusted gross income ($63,825) is $52,225 (Line 41).
- There are five exemptions. The exemption amount is $3,700. The total deduction for exemptions is $18,500 ($3,700 multiplied by 5) (Line 42).
- Taxable income is $33,725 (Line 43).

The standard deduction is increased for taxpayers and spouses who are age 65 or older or blind. The standard deduction may be reduced for a taxpayer who can be claimed as a dependent on another taxpayer's return. For 2011, the standard deduction for a taxpayer who can be claimed as a dependent on another taxpayer's return is calculated thusly:

6

Form 1040 (2011) Page **2**

	Line	Description		Line	Amount
Tax and Credits	38	Amount from line 37 (adjusted gross income)		38	68,825 00
	39a	Check if: ☐ **You** were born before January 2, 1947, ☐ Blind. / ☐ **Spouse** was born before January 2, 1947, ☐ Blind. **Total boxes checked ▶ 39a** ☐			
Standard Deduction for—	b	If your spouse itemizes on a separate return or you were a dual-status alien, check here▶ 39b☐			
• People who check any box on line 39a or 39b **or** who can be claimed as a dependent, see instructions.	40	**Itemized deductions** (from Schedule A) **or** your **standard deduction** (see left margin)		40	11,600 00
	41	Subtract line 40 from line 38		41	52,225 00
	42	**Exemptions.** Multiply $3,700 by the number on line 6d		42	18,500 00
	43	**Taxable income.** Subtract line 42 from line 41. If line 42 is more than line 41, enter -0-		43	33,725 00
	44	**Tax** (see instructions). Check if any from: **a** ☐ Form(s) 8814 **b** ☐ Form 4972 **c** ☐ 962 election		44	
	45	**Alternative minimum tax** (see instructions). Attach Form 6251		45	
	46	Add lines 44 and 45 ▶		46	
• All others: Single or Married filing separately, $5,800	47	Foreign tax credit. Attach Form 1116 if required	47		
	48	Credit for child and dependent care expenses. Attach Form 2441	48		
	49	Education credits from Form 8863, line 23	49		
Married filing jointly or Qualifying widow(er), $11,600	50	Retirement savings contributions credit. Attach Form 8880	50		
	51	Child tax credit (see instructions)	51		
	52	Residential energy credits. Attach Form 5695	52		
Head of household, $8,500	53	Other credits from Form: **a** ☐ 3800 **b** ☐ 8801 **c** ☐	53		
	54	Add lines 47 through 53. These are your **total credits**		54	
	55	Subtract line 54 from line 46. If line 54 is more than line 46, enter -0- ▶		55	
Other Taxes	56	Self-employment tax. Attach Schedule SE		56	
	57	Unreported social security and Medicare tax from Form: **a** ☐ 4137 **b** ☐ 8919		57	
	58	Additional tax on IRAs, other qualified retirement plans, etc. Attach Form 5329 if required		58	
	59a	Household employment taxes from Schedule H		59a	
	b	First-time homebuyer credit repayment. Attach Form 5405 if required		59b	
	60	Other taxes. Enter code(s) from instructions		60	
	61	Add lines 55 through 60. This is your **total tax** ▶		61	

Figure 6-1 Tax and Credit Section IRS Form 1040A Standard Deduction

- Earned income (wages, salaries, tips, and so forth) plus $300
- But not less than $950
- And not more than the standard deduction for the single filing status ($5,800)

Review the tax and credits section of Irene Ketchum's tax return (see Figure 6-2). Irene is single and is claimed as a dependent on her parents' tax return. She is 18 years old. She had interest income of $400 and wages of $4,350.

- The adjusted gross income is $4,750 ($400 + $4,350) (Line 38).
- The standard deduction is $4,650 (earned income of $4,350 + $300) (Line 40).
- The standard deduction ($4,650) subtracted from the adjusted gross income ($4, 750) is $100 (Line 41).
- Irene cannot claim an exemption for herself because she is claimed as a dependent on her parents' return (Line 42).
- Taxable income is $100 (Internal Revenue Service, n.d. [h]).

If you are a dependent, it's wise to check with your parents before filing your tax return.

Figure 6-2 Tax and Credit Section IRS Form 1040A Standard Deduction without Exemption (Dependent)

TAX CREDITS

A **tax credit** is another benefit to taxpayers to help them limit their tax liability. Tax credits are dollar-for-dollar reductions in the taxes that can be deducted directly from any taxes owed.

▶ **CHILD TAX CREDIT AND ADDITIONAL CHILD TAX CREDIT.** The child tax credit allows taxpayers to claim a tax credit of up to $1,000 per qualifying child under the age of 17. This reduces their tax liability, potentially to $0. To claim the credit, the taxpayer and child must meet numerous requirements. A **nonrefundable tax credit** allows taxpayers to lower their tax liability to zero, but not below zero. The child tax credit is nonrefundable.

When a taxpayer's child tax credit is more than their tax liability, they may be eligible to claim an additional child tax credit as well as the child tax credit. The additional tax credit is for certain individuals who get less than the full amount of the child tax credit. The additional child tax credit may give a taxpayer a refund even if they do not owe any tax. Taxpayers must meet additional requirements to claim this credit. A **refundable tax credit** allows taxpayers to lower their tax liability to zero and still receive a refund. The additional child tax credit is refundable.

▶ **TAX CREDIT FOR CHILD AND DEPENDENT CARE EXPENSES.** The tax credit for child and dependent care expenses allows taxpayers to claim a credit for expenses paid for the care of children under age 13 and for a disabled spouse or dependent. To claim the credit, taxpayers must meet numerous requirements for the taxpayer, the expenses, and the qualifying person. There is a limit to the amount of qualifying expenses. The credit is a percentage of the qualifying expenses (Internal Revenue Service, n.d. [j]).

▶ **EDUCATION CREDITS.** Taxpayers have two credits available to help offset the costs of higher education. These credits are the American Opportunity Credit and Lifetime Learning Credit, also referred to collectively as education credits. The requirements for taking these credits depend on the following:

- Filing status and adjusted gross income or modified gross income of the taxpayer.

- Eligible education institution. Eligible education institutions include any college, university, vocational school, or other postsecondary educational institution eligible to participate in a student aid program administered by the Department of Education. Virtually all accredited public, nonprofit, and proprietary (privately owned profit-making) postsecondary institutions are included.

- Qualified tuition and related expenses. Related expenses are defined as course-related books and materials, supplies and equipment, and activities.

The American Opportunity Credit (previously known as the Hope Credit) allows taxpayers to claim a credit of up to $2,500, part of which may be refundable. Taxpayers may claim a Lifetime Learning Credit of up to $2,000.

Differences between the Two Credits

The amount of the American Opportunity Credit is gradually reduced as taxpayers' income increases.

There is no limit on the number of years the Lifetime Learning Credit can be claimed.

The differences between the two credits are summarized in the following chart.

Lifetime Learning Credit	American Opportunity Credit
Up to $2,000 credit per return	Up to $2,500 credit per eligible student
Available for an unlimited number of years	Available *only* for the first four years of postsecondary education
Credit available for courses taken as part of a postsecondary degree program or to acquire or improve job skills (including noncredit courses and graduate-level work)	Must be pursuing a degree or other educational credential
Available for one or more courses	Must take at least half of the normal full-time workload for one academic period
Felony drug convictions rule does not apply	Felony drug conviction restriction
Credit is nonrefundable	40% of credit is refundable

A taxpayer cannot claim any of the following:

- A deduction for higher education expenses and also claim an American Opportunity or Lifetime Learning Credit based on those same expenses
- Both American Opportunity Credit and a Lifetime Learning Credit for the same student in the same year
- A credit based on expenses paid with a tax-free scholarship, grant, or employer-provided educational assistance

The American Opportunity and Lifetime Learning Credits are claimed on Form 8863, which can be filed with either Form 1040 or Form 1040A (Internal Revenue Service, n.d. [k]).

▶ **EARNED INCOME CREDIT.** The earned income credit is a refundable tax credit for people who work and whose earned income and adjusted gross income are under a specific limit. Many rules apply to the earned income credit, including a limit on the amount of investment income. Generally, the taxpayer's earned income, filing status, and number of qualifying children, if any, determine the credit. Eligible taxpayers can receive the earned income credit even if their tax is zero (Internal Revenue Service, n.d. [l]).

ELECTRONIC TAX RETURN PREPARATION AND TRANSMISSION

Prior to the arrival of the Internet, doing one's taxes was a manual and laborious process that required considerable time and effort by the preparer (either the taxpayer or an outside entity such as an accountant or a tax advisor). While many people still choose to prepare and transmit their taxes manually, the Internal Revenue Service reports that today, eight out of ten filers opt to file their returns electronically (also known as **IRS e-filing**). Regardless of which method you choose, doing your taxes involves two phases: tax preparation and tax transmission.

1040

NOTE: THIS BOOKLET DOES NOT CONTAIN TAX FORMS

INSTRUCTIONS

2011

 makes doing your taxes faster and easier.

 is the fast, safe, and free way to prepare and *e-file* your taxes. See *www.irs.gov/freefile.*

Get a faster refund, reduce errors, and save paper. For more information on **IRS** *e-file* and Free File, see Options for *e-filing* your returns in these instructions or click on **IRS** *e-file* at IRS.gov.

NEW FORMS

You may have to report your capital gains and losses on new Form 8949 and report the totals on Schedule D. If you have foreign financial assets, you may have to file new Form 8938.

MAILING YOUR RETURN

If you file a paper return, you may be mailing it to a different address this year.

FUTURE DEVELOPMENTS

The IRS has created a page on IRS.gov for information about Form 1040 and its instructions at *www.irs.gov/form1040.* Information about any future developments affecting Form 1040 (such as legislation enacted after we release it) will be posted on that page.

For details on these and other changes, see *What's New* in these instructions.

IRS

Department of the Treasury **Internal Revenue Service** IRS.gov

Internal Revenue Service

Nov 28, 2011   Cat. No. 24811V

Helpful online instructions such as these from the Internal Revenue Service make "e-filing" a streamlined process.

TAX PREPARATION

Tax preparation means the completion of all the forms and schedules (attachments) needed to compute and report the tax. Returns can be prepared manually or electronically.

Electronic preparation of tax returns has the following advantages:

▶ **INCREASED ACCURACY.** An important benefit of the electronic preparation of tax returns is the reduction of errors. The error rate in electronically prepared returns is significantly lower than that of manually prepared returns.

▶ **EASE OF USE.** Tax-preparation software is easy to use. Most tax-preparation software uses expert systems, known as wizards, to help with return preparation. The wizard guides the preparer through the steps of completing the tax return.

▶ **ABILITY TO PREPARE FEDERAL AND STATE RETURNS AT THE SAME TIME.** Using tax-preparation software, many taxpayers can prepare both federal and state returns at the same time.

Electronic tax preparation options include the following:

- **Online, self-prepared**. Taxpayers use a personal computer to prepare and transmit tax returns via the Internet. Expert systems (often called wizards) provided in tax software guide taxpayers through the process. Taxpayers then sign the return with a self-selected personal identification number (PIN) and transmit the return over the Internet (more information on PINs follows). Taxpayers may prepare and transmit their tax forms from home, the workplace (as an employer-provided benefit), the local library (usually free), a financial institution (usually free), or a business (usually for a fee).

- **Authorized IRS e-file Provider.** An **Authorized IRS e-file Provider** is a business authorized by the IRS to participate in the IRS e-file Program. The business may be a sole proprietorship, a partnership, a corporation, or an organization. Authorized IRS e-file Providers include the following:

  - **Electronic Return Originator (ERO).** The Authorized IRS e-file Provider that originates the electronic submission of an income tax return to the IRS. EROs may originate the electronic submission of income tax returns they either prepared or collected from taxpayers. Some EROs charge a fee for submitting returns electronically. Often EROs also prepare returns. EROs include the following:

- Certified Public Accountants (CPAs)
- Tax attorneys
- IRS enrolled agents (individuals who are registered with the IRS)
- Tax-preparation businesses
- VITA (Volunteer Income Tax Assistance) sites, as sponsored by the IRS
- TCE (Tax Counseling for the Elderly) sites operated by the American Association of Retired Persons (AARP)
- Walk-in sites

- **Transmitter.** Sends the electronic return data directly to the IRS
- **Intermediate service provider.** Assists in processing tax return information between the ERO (or the taxpayer, in the case of online filing) and the transmitter
- **Software developer.** Develops software for the purposes of (1) formatting electronic tax return information according to IRS specifications and/or (2) transmitting electronic tax return information directly to the IRS

These categories are not mutually exclusive. For example, an ERO can at the same time be a transmitter, a software developer, or an intermediate service provider, depending on the function being performed.

TAX TRANSMISSION

Tax transmission means sending the tax return to the taxing authority. As with tax preparation, returns can be transmitted by mail or electronically.

There are significant advantages to transmitting tax returns electronically:

▶ **ACCURACY.** Your chances of getting an error notice are significantly reduced.

▶ **PAPERLESS WITH THE SELF-SELECT PERSONAL IDENTIFICATION NUMBER (PIN) OPTION.** Electronic filing reduces the paper used to file tax returns. It is environmentally friendly. A taxpayer creates his or her own PIN and files a completely paperless return.

▶ **SECURE.** With electronic filing, taxpayer privacy and security are ensured. Personal identification numbers (PINs) ensure that the taxpayer, and not someone else, transmitted each tax return. A PIN allows the taxpayer to "sign" the return electronically. Most taxpayers can qualify to use a PIN by providing their date of birth and adjusted gross income from their originally filed prior year tax return.

▶ **ELECTRONIC ACKNOWLEDGMENT.** Within 48 hours of transmission, the IRS sends an electronic acknowledgment that the return was received and accepted for processing.

▶ **DIRECT DEPOSIT FOR FASTER REFUNDS.** Taxpayers who file electronically receive refunds faster than those who transmit returns through the mail. If the taxpayer chooses the direct deposit option, the refund is received in less than half the time of a mailed return. E-filers who choose direct deposit can receive their refund in as few as 10 days.

▶ **FREE OR LOW-COST FILING.** Free or low-cost filing options are available to qualified taxpayers. Check out the IRS Web site at www.irs.gov to see if you qualify.

▶ **ELECTRONIC FUNDS WITHDRAWAL FOR PAYMENTS.** Taxpayers who file electronically can arrange to have the balance due paid by scheduling an electronic funds withdrawal from their checking or savings accounts. A taxpayer with a balance due can file his or her tax return early and arrange to have the funds paid later (up to 10 days before the due date of the tax return) or pay by credit card.

▶ **ABLE TO TRANSMIT FEDERAL AND STATE TAXES AT THE SAME TIME.** Prepare and file both federal and state returns together, and double the benefits you get from e-file. Thirty-six states and the District of Columbia participate in the Federal/State e-file Program.

Transmission can be one of the following:

- Through the mail
- Through electronic filing (e-file) options:
  - Online, self-prepared

- Authorized IRS e-file Provider
- Volunteer Income Tax Assistance (VITA) sites
- TCE (Tax Counseling for the Elderly) sites operated by AARP
- Paid tax preparers (Internal Revenue Service, n.d. [m]).

CONSEQUENCES OF NOT PAYING TAXES

As a responsible citizen, it is your duty to file your yearly individual tax return based on the rules and regulations set forth by the U.S. Constitution and administered and enforced by the Internal Revenue Service. And, like you, the vast majority of people who are required to file taxes do so in a timely manner and pay what is owed without incident.

One of the smartest things you can do to make sure you file your return on time (April 15 each year) is to keep accurate records. Good records can help you do the following:

▶ Identify sources of income.

▶ Keep track of expenses.

▶ Prepare tax returns quickly and easily.

▶ Support items on tax returns.

▶ Keep track of the basis of property (Internal Revenue Service, n.d. [n]).

You should get into the habit of keeping your financial records in order and staying with that good habit for the rest of your life.

If you are not able to complete your tax return by the deadline, the IRS makes provisions for getting an extension (to October 15 of the same year) for filing. Do note, however, that if you owe any money, you must send it with the extension form by the April 15 deadline.

If you deliberately and willfully hide income from the IRS, falsely claim deductions, or otherwise cheat the government out of taxes it is owed (for example, not paying your taxes at all), you are committing **tax evasion**. Tax evasion is illegal and the consequences are dire, including penalties, fines, interest charges, and a possible jail sentence. A financially literate person knows that being a responsible taxpayer does not include any form of tax evasion!

CASE IN POINT REVISITED

In the Case in Point presented at the beginning of this chapter, Spencer Burns received payroll tax information from his employer after the first of the year, but he was unsure of what to do with the form, so he ignored it. Fortunately for Spencer, his parents came to visit him at school before the April 15 deadline for filing taxes and inquired as to whether he had already filed.

Upon hearing this news, Spencer's dad walked him through the process by going to the Internal Revenue Service's Web site (www.irs.gov) to retrieve the needed form and helped Spencer fill out the required information. Spencer then sent the form in electronically and was delighted to learn that he was actually getting a tax refund.

CHAPTER SUMMARY

Chapter 6 provided an introduction to individual taxes. Concepts covered included understanding your obligations and responsibilities as a taxpayer, identifying the components of tax reporting, and the mechanics of electronic tax form preparation and transmission. The consequences of not paying one's taxes concluded the chapter.

POINTS TO KEEP IN MIND

▶ The Internal Revenue Service is responsible for administering and enforcing the Internal Revenue Code.

▶ Taxes provide revenue for federal, local, and state governments to fund essential services.

▶ The U.S. income tax system is built on the idea of voluntary compliance.

▶ Transaction taxes come from the sale of goods and services, income taxes come from taxes on earned and unearned income, and property taxes come from taxes on property.

▶ Tax liability is your tax bill for the year.

▶ Payroll taxes consist of Social Security tax and Medicare tax.

▶ Employers are required by law to send employees a W-2, Wage and Tax Statement, by January 31 of the following year.

▶ Tips are taxable and need to be reported on the taxpayer's individual income tax return.

▶ There are five different filing statuses. Most taxpayers choose the one that results in the lowest tax payment.

▶ There are two types of tax exemptions: personal and dependency.

▶ A standard deduction reduces the income subject to tax. For most taxpayers, a standard deduction is based on filing status.

▶ A tax credit is benefit to taxpayers to help them limit their tax liability. There are several different types of tax credits.

▶ Eight out of ten tax filers prepare and transmit their returns electronically.

▶ Good recordkeeping is important when it comes to preparing a tax return.

▶ Tax evasion is illegal and carries significant financial and personal ramifications.

6

CRITICAL THINKING QUESTIONS

1. There are many advantages to preparing and transmitting tax returns electronically. Name as many as you can.

2. Why might it be important to itemize your deductions instead of using the standard deduction on your tax return?

3. When it comes to taxes, why is financial recordkeeping so important?

4. Have you knowingly or unknowingly been a contributor to the "underground economy"?

5. If you have never filed a tax return before, from whom might you seek advice?

apply it!

Activity #1: Understanding Education Credits

GOAL: Help you figure out if you or your parents can claim an education credit on an individual income tax return.

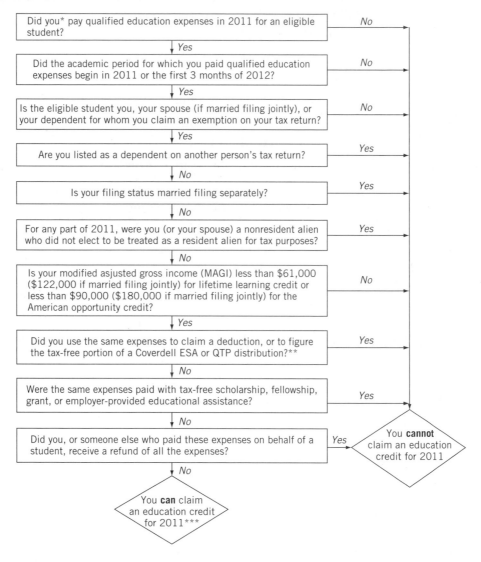

*Qualified education expenses paid by a dependent for whom you claim an exemption, or by a third party for that dependent, are considered paid by you.

**You cannot use the same expenses to claim both a lifetime learning credit and an American opportunity credit.

***Your education credits may be limited to your tax liability minus certain credits. See Form 8863 for more details.

STEP 1: As a class, and using the Education Credit Flowchart on the preceding page, walk through the steps in the flowchart.

STEP 2: Determine if you or your parents are eligible to claim an education credit on an individual income tax return.

CHECK YOUR UNDERSTANDING

Visit www.cengagebrain.com to see how well you have mastered the material in Chapter 6.

REFERENCES

Internal Revenue Service (n.d.[a]). *Why pay taxes?* Retrieved February 27, 2012, from www.irs.gov/app/understandingTaxes/whys/thm01/les01/media/lp_thm01_les01.pdf

Internal Revenue Service (n.d. [b]). *Federal/state/local taxes.* Retrieved February 27, 2012, from www.irs.gov/app/understandingTaxes/teacher/whys_thm04_les01.jsp

Internal Revenue Service (n.d. [c]). *Income tax facts.* Retrieved February 28, 2012, from www.irs.gov/app/understandingTaxes/whys/thm04/les03/media/is1_thm04_les03.pdf

Internal Revenue Service (n.d. [d]). *Payroll taxes and federal income tax withholding.* Retrieved February 28, 2012, from www.irs.gov/app/understandingTaxes/hows/mod01/media/lp_mod01.pdf

Internal Revenue Service (n.d. [e]). *Wage and tip income.* Retrieved February 28, 2012, from www.irs.gov/app/understandingTaxes/teacher/hows_mod02.jsp

Internal Revenue Service (n.d. [f]). *Interest income.* Retrieved February 28, 2012, from www.irs.gov/app/understandingTaxes/hows/mod03/media/lp_mod03.pdf

Internal Revenue Service (n.d. [g]). *Exemptions.* Retrieved February 29, 2012, from www.irs.gov/app/understandingTaxes/teacher/hows_mod06.jsp

Internal Revenue Service (n.d. [h]). *Standard deduction.* Retrieved February 29, 2012, from www.irs.gov/app/understandingTaxes/teacher/hows_mod07.jsp

Internal Revenue Service (n.d. [i]). *Child tax credit and additional child tax credit*. Retrieved February 29, 2012, from www.irs.gov/app/understandingTaxes/hows/mod08/media/lp_mod08.pdf

Internal Revenue Service (n.d. [j]. *Tax credit for child and dependent care expenses*. Retrieved February 29, 2012, from www.irs.gov/app/understandingTaxes/teacher/hows_mod09.jsp

Internal Revenue Service (n.d. [k]). *Education credits*. Retrieved February 29, 2012, from www.irs.gov/app/understandingTaxes/teacher/hows_mod10.jsp

Internal Revenue Service (n.d. [l]). *Earned income credit*. Retrieved February 29, 2012, from www.irs.gov/app/understandingTaxes/teacher/hows_mod11.jsp

Internal Revenue Service (n.d. [m]). *Electronic tax return preparation and transmission*. Retrieved March 1, 2012, from www.irs.gov/app/understandingTaxes/teacher/hows_mod13.jsp

Internal Revenue Service (n.d. [n]). *Refund, amount due, and recordkeeping*. Retrieved March 1, 2012, from www.irs.gov/app/understandingTaxes/teacher/hows_mod12.jsp

6

Appendix A
Financial Literacy
Web Sites

BANKING SITES

www.bankrate.com – This site offers mortgage rates, home loans, refinancing, credit cards, and CD rates with personal finance advice. It also has a wide variety of calculators.

www.depositaccounts.com – This site lists the best rates on different types of deposit accounts (savings, CDs, regular banks, and money markets).

www.mycreditunion.gov – This is a consumer-based web site about credit unions.

www.savingsaccounts.com – This site lists the best deals on savings accounts rates.

CREDIT REPORTS/SCORES/CREDIT COUNSELING

www.annualcreditreport.com – This central site allows you to request a free credit file disclosure, commonly called a credit report, once every 12 months from each of the nationwide consumer credit reporting companies: Equifax, Experian, and TransUnion.

www.consumercreditcounseling.com – This is a nonprofit group that offers counseling on your finances.

www.freescoreonline.com – This site offers free credit scores from the big three credit bureaus with a seven-day trial.

www.moneymanagement.org – Money Management International (MMI) is the largest nonprofit, full-service credit counseling agency in the United States. They provide professional financial guidance, credit counseling, communitywide educational programs, debt management assistance, bankruptcy counseling and education services, and housing counseling assistance to consumers via phone, Internet, and in-person sessions.

FINANCIAL AID/STUDENT LOANS

www.direct.ed.gov – This is the home page of the U.S. Department of Education's Direct Loan Program.

www.ed.gov – The United States Department of Education site offers several financial aid guides for consumers.

www.nasfaa.org – The National Association of Student Financial Aid Administrators provides a "Cash for College Guide" with advice, tips, and information on financing an education.

www.nslds.ed.gov – The National Student Loan Data System provides information about all of your Direct Loans, FFEL Program Loans, and Federal Perkins Loans.

www.studentaid.ed.gov – This site provides online resources that cover the full range of financial aid topics, from preparing for a college education all the way through repaying student loans.

TAXES

www.irs.gov/individuals/students/topic/index.html – This site provides tax information for students.

Glossary

401 (k) plan Defined-contribution plan designed for employees of private corporations.

A

Adjusted gross income Total income reduced by certain amounts, such as for an IRA or student loan interest.

Aesthetics The quality of being creatively, beautifully, or artistically pleasing; aesthetic needs are the needs to express oneself in pleasing ways.

All-in-one account *See* Asset management account.

Annual Percentage Rate (APR) The measure of the cost of credit, expressed as a yearly interest rate.

Asset management account (AMA) *See also* All-in-one account and Central asset account. Multipurpose, coordinated package that gathers most monetary asset vehicles into a unified account and reports activity on a single monthly statement to the client.

Authorized IRS e-file Provider A business authorized by the IRS to participate in the IRS e-file Program. The business may be a sole proprietorship, a partnership, a corporation, or an organization. Authorized IRS e-file Providers include Electronic Return Originators (EROs), Transmitters, Intermediate Service Providers, and Software Developers. These categories are not mutually exclusive. For example, an ERO can at the same time, be a Transmitter, a Software Developer, or an Intermediate Service Provider, depending on the function being performed.

Automated Clearing House (ACH) An electronic network for financial transactions in the United States.

B

Bonus Compensation received by an employee for services performed. A bonus is given in addition to an employee's usual compensation.

Bounced check Writing a check for more money than you have in your account.

Budget A paper or electronic document used to record both planned and actual income and expenditures over a period of time.

Business bank *See* Commercial bank.

C

Campus-Based Aid Federal student aid loans paid directly to you through your school's financial aid office.

Capitalization Adding unpaid interest to the loan principal on a student loan. Capitalization increases the principal amount of the loan and its total cost.

Capital market A market in which individuals and institutions trade financial securities.

Central asset account *See* Asset management account.

Certificate of deposit (CD) An interest-earnings savings instrument purchased for a fixed period of time.

Commercial bank A bank that only has a financial relationship with businesses.

Commission Like salaries and wages, commissions are compensation received by an employee for services performed. Commissions are paid based on a percentage of sales made or a fixed amount per sale.

Compound interest When interest on an investment (such as money in a savings account) itself earns interest.

Contribution plan An employee-sponsored retirement plan that accepts employee as well as employer contributions. A 401 (k) plan is an example of a contribution plan.

Credit A term used to describe an arrangement in which goods, services, or money is received in exchange for a promise to repay at a future date.

Creditor A company who lends money or services.

Credit bureau Firm that collects and keeps records of many borrowers' credit histories.

Credit history Continuing record of a person's credit usage and repayment of debts.

Credit limit *See* Spending limit.

Credit report Information compiled by a credit bureau from merchants, utility companies, banks, court records, and creditors about your payment history.

Credit score Statistical measure used to rate applicants based on various factors deemed relevant to creditworthiness and the likelihood of repayment.

Credit union (CU) A member-owned, not-for-profit federally insured financial institution that provides checking, savings, and loan services to members.

D

Deferment A temporary suspension of loan payments for specific situations such as reenrollment in school, unemployment, or economic hardship.

Dependency exemption Can be claimed for those who pass the dependency tests for qualifying child or qualifying relative. Each dependency exemption reduces the income subject to tax by the exemption amount. The exemption amount changes yearly.

Deposit account A type of savings account, which can be in the form of a traditional savings account, a certificate of deposit (CD), or a money market account.

Discretionary income Money left over after necessities such as housing and food are paid for.

E

Electronic Return Originator (ERO) Authorized IRS e-file Provider that originates the electronic submission of an income tax return to the IRS. EROs may originate the electronic submission of income tax returns they either prepared or collected from taxpayers. Some EROs charge a fee for submitting returns electronically.

Exemption amount A set amount that changes from year to year. For 2011, for example, the amount was $3,700. Each exemption reduces the income subject to tax by the exemption amount.

Exemptions Amounts that taxpayers can claim for themselves, their spouses, and eligible dependents. There are two types of exemptions—personal and dependency. Each exemption reduces the income subject to tax. While each is worth the same amount, different rules apply to each type.

Expected Family Contribution (EFC) The number used to determine eligibility for federal student financial aid. This number results from the financial information provided on the FAFSA application. The EFC is reported on the Student Aid Report (SAR).

Exit counseling For borrowers of federal or Direct student loans, a federal regulation that applies to all students who have graduated, officially withdrawn, dropped below half-time enrollment, transferred to another institution, or simply ceased attendance.

F

Federal income tax The federal government levies a tax on personal income. The federal income tax provides for national programs such as defense, foreign affairs, law enforcement, and interest on the national debt.

Federal Insurance Contributions Act (FICA) *See* Social Security taxes.

Filing status Determines the rate at which income is taxed. The five filing statuses are: single, married filing jointly, married filing separately, head of household, and qualifying widow(er) with dependent child.

Financial aid Any form of financial assistance from any number of sources.

Financial aid administrator (FAA) An individual who works at a college or career school and is responsible for preparing and communicating information on student loans, grants or scholarships, and employment programs.

Financial education The process by which people improve their understanding of financial products, services, and concepts so they are empowered to make informed choices, avoid pitfalls, know where to go for help, and take other actions to improve their present and long-term financial well-being.

Financial goals Specific objectives addressed by planning and managing finances.

Financially illiterate The inability to understand one's personal financial situation and the consequences that arise from making poor financial decisions.

Financial literacy The ability to use knowledge and skills to manage financial resources effectively for a lifetime of financial well-being.

Financial planner An investment professional who helps individuals set and achieve their long-term financial goals.

Forbearance A temporary postponement of payments, temporary ability to make smaller payments, or extension of the time for making payments.

Form W-4, Employee's Withholding Allowance Certificate Completed by the employee and used by the employer to determine the amount of income tax to withhold.

Free Application for Federal Student Aid (FAFSA) Required form (both electronic and print versions) used by the federal government to determine need when awarding federal student aid.

G

Goal The purpose toward which an endeavor is directed.

Grace period The time between the date of the credit card purchase and the date the company starts charging interest. In the case of repaying student loans, a six-month period before the first payment must be made on a subsidized or unsubsidized Stafford loan. Interest is accrued on the loan during the grace period. The grace period begins the day after the borrower ceases to be enrolled at least half time (including graduation).

Gross income The amount paid to the employee before any taxes or other contributions are deducted.

H

Head of Household filing status Must meet the following requirements: (1) You are unmarried or considered unmarried on the last day of the year. (2) You paid more than half the cost of keeping up a home for the year. (3) A qualifying person lived with you in the home for more than half the year (except temporary absences, such as school). However, your dependent parent does not have to live with you.

I

Income taxes Taxes on income, both earned (salaries, wages, tips, commissions) and unearned (interest, dividends). Income taxes can be levied both on individuals (personal income taxes) and businesses (business and corporate income taxes).

Individual Retirement Account (IRA) Investment accounts that reduce current year income and that are allowed to accumulate tax free.

Inflation A steady and sustained rise in general price levels across economic sectors; measured by the changing cost over time of a "market basket" of goods and services that a typical household might purchase.

Interest Charge for borrowing money; investors in bonds earn interest.

Intermediate Service Provider Assists in processing tax return information between the ERO (or the taxpayer, in the case of online filing) and the Transmitter.

Investment Tangible and intangible items acquired for their monetary benefits.

Investment bank A financial institution that deals only with capital markets.

Internal Revenue Code The statutory tax law of the United States as administered by the Internal Revenue Service (IRS).

Internal Revenue Service (IRS) A bureau of the U.S. Department of the Treasury responsible for collecting taxes and the interpretation and enforcement of the Internal Revenue Code.

IRS e-file The preparation and transmission of tax return information to the IRS using a computer with a modem or Internet access.

M

Married Filing Jointly filing status You are married and both you and your spouse agree to file a joint return. (On a joint return, you report your combined income and deduct your combined allowable expenses.)

Married Filing Separately filing status You must be married. This method may benefit you if you want to be responsible only for your own tax or if this method results in less tax than a joint return. If you and your spouse do not agree to file a joint return, you may have to use this filing status.

Master Promissory Note (MPN) A legal document in which you promise to repay your Direct Stafford loan and any accrued interest and fees to the U.S. Department of Education.

Matching contribution Employer benefit that offers a full or partial matching contribution to a participating employee's account in proportion to each dollar of contributions made by the participant.

Medicare tax Used to provide medical benefits for certain individuals when they reach age 65. Workers, retired workers, and the spouses of workers and retired workers are eligible to received Medicare benefits upon reaching age 65.

Money market account An interest-earning account that pays relatively high interest rates and offers limited check-writing privileges.

Money Market Deposit Account (MMDA) Government-insured money market account with minimum balance requirements and tiered interest rates.

Money Market Mutual Fund (MMMF) Money market account in a mutual fund rather than at a depository institution.

N

Need Something that is a necessity in life, such as food, water, and shelter.

Net income Income realized after employer withholding for taxes and insurance.

Negotiable Order of Withdrawal (NOW) Account An interest-earning bank account with which the customer is permitted to write drafts against money held on deposit.

Nonrefundable Tax Credit Allows taxpayers to lower their tax liability to zero, but not below zero.

P

Payday advance *See* Payday loan.

Payday loan A small, short-term loan that is intended to cover a borrower's expenses until his or her next payday (also called a paycheck advance).

Payroll taxes Include Social Security (or FICA) and Medicare taxes.

Pension Sum of money paid regularly as a retirement benefit.

Personal exemption(s) Can be claimed for the taxpayer and spouse.

Personal identification number (PIN) Allows taxpayers to "sign" their tax returns electronically. The PIN, a five-digit self-selected number, ensures that electronically submitted tax returns are authentic. Most taxpayers can qualify to use a PIN.

Personal responsibility Working on our own character and skill development rather than blaming others for situations and circumstances.

Personal values The principles, standards, or qualities considered worthwhile or desirable.

Principal Face amount of a bond or the price originally paid for a bond.

Property taxes Taxes on property, especially real estate, but also can be on boats, automobiles (often paid along with license fees), recreational vehicles, and business inventories.

Public goods and services Benefits that cannot be withheld from those who don't pay for them and benefits that may be "consumed" by one person without reducing the amount of the product available for others. Examples include national defense, streetlights, and roads and highways. Public services include welfare programs, law enforcement, and monitoring and regulating trade and the economy.

Q

Qualifying Widow(er) with Dependent Child filing status If your spouse died in 2011, for example, you could have used married filing jointly as your filing status for 2011 if you otherwise qualified to use that status. The year of death is the last year for which you can file jointly with your described spouse. You may be eligible to use qualifying widow(er) with dependent child as your filing status for two years following the year of death of your spouse.

R

Refund Money owed to taxpayers when their total tax payments are greater than the total tax liability.

Refundable tax credit Allows taxpayers to lower their tax liability to zero and still receive a refund.

Retail bank Financial institution that caters primarily to individuals.

Retirement The time in life when the major sources of income change from earned income (such as a salary or wages) to employer-based retirement benefits, private savings and investments, income from Social Security, and perhaps part-time employment.

S

Salary Compensation received by an employee for services performed. A salary is a fixed sum paid for a specific period of time worked, such as weekly or monthly.

Savings account An account that provides an accessible source of emergency cash and a temporary holding place for extra funds that will earn some interest.

Savings and loan institution A type of bank that primarily provides financing for long-term residential mortgages.

Self-actualization A person's desire to become everything he or she is capable of becoming—to realize and use his or her full potential, capacities, and talents.

Single filing status If on the last day of the year, you are unmarried or legally separated from your spouse under a divorce or separate maintenance decree and you do not qualify for another filing status.

Social Security statement A document that the Social Security Administration periodically sends to all workers that includes earnings history, Social Security taxes paid, and an estimated benefits amount.

Social Security taxes Provide benefits for retired workers and their dependents as well as for the disabled and their dependents, also known as Federal Insurance Contributions Act (FICA).

Software developer Develops software for the purposes of (1) formatting electronic tax return information according to IRS specifications, and/or (2) transmitting electronic tax return information directly to the IRS.

Spending limit The maximum outstanding debt that a lender will allow on an open-ended credit account.

Standard deduction Reduces the income subject to tax and varies depending on filing status, age, blindness, and dependency.

Student Aid Report (SAR) FAFSA results that are either sent in an e-mail report within a few days after the FAFSA has been processed or by mail in a few weeks, depending on how the application was originally completed (online or paper, respectively).

Super NOW account A high-interest Negotiable Order of Withdrawal (NOW) account.

T

Tax credit A dollar-for-dollar reduction in the tax. Can be deducted directly from taxes owed.

Tax deduction An amount (often a personal or business expense) that reduces income subject to tax.

Tax deferral The individual does not have to pay current income taxes on the earnings (interest, dividends, and capital gains) reinvested in a retirement account.

Tax evasion Deliberately and willfully hiding income from the IRS, falsely claiming deductions, or otherwise cheating the government out of taxes owed; it is illegal.

Taxable interest income The income a person receives from certain bank accounts or from lending money to someone else.

Tax credit Dollar-for-dollar reduction in the tax that can be deducted directly from any taxes owed.

Tax-exempt interest income Income that is not subject to income tax and is earned on funds loaned to states, cities, counties, or the District of Columbia.

Tax liability (or total tax bill) The amount of tax that must be paid. Taxpayers meet (or pay) their federal income tax liability through withholding, estimated tax payments, and payments made with the tax forms they file with the government.

Tax preparation The completion of all the forms and schedules needed to compute and report the tax.

Tax transmission Sending the tax return to the taxing authority.

Tip income Money and goods received for services performed by food servers, baggage handlers, babysitters, hairdressers, and others. Tips go beyond the stated amount of the bill and are given voluntarily.

Transaction taxes Taxes on economic transactions, such as the sale of goods and services. These can be based on a set of percentages of the sales value (sales taxes), or they can be a set amount on physical quantities ("per unit"—gasoline taxes).

Transmitter Sends the electronic return data directly to the IRS.

U

Underground economy Money-making activities that people don't report to the government, including both illegal and legal activities.

V

Voluntary compliance A system of compliance that relies on individual citizens to report their income freely and voluntarily, calculate their tax liability correctly, and file a tax return on time.

W

Wages Compensation received by employees for services performed. Usually, wages are computed by multiplying an hourly rate by the number of hours worked.

Want Something that is not a necessity but is desired to increase the quality of life.

Withholding ("pay-as-you-earn" taxation) Money, for example, that employers withhold from employees' paychecks. This money is deposited for the government. (It will be credited against the employees' tax liability when they file their returns.) Employers withhold money for federal income taxes, Social Security taxes, and state and local income taxes in some states and localities.

Y

Yield Annual rate of return on an investment.

Index